WHAT WE TALK ABOUT WHEN WE TALK ABOUT CITIES (AND LOVE)

WHAT WE TALK ABOUT WHEN WE TALK ABOUT CITIES (AND LOVE)

ANDY MERRIFIELD

OR Books
New York · London

Published by OR Books, New York and London
Visit our website at www.orbooks.com

First printing 2018.

Cataloging-in-Publication data is available from the Library of Congress.
A catalog record for this book is available from the British Library.

Typeset by Lapiz Digital Services, Chennai, India. Printed by BookMobile in the United States and CPI Books Ltd in the United Kingdom.

Paperback ISBN 978-1-682191-43-9 • ebook ISBN 978-1-682191-44-6

For C.

& heartfelt thanks to Colin R.

"I mean, I'm just talking, right?"
—Raymond Carver

I've read and admired plenty of short stories from plenty of great writers but there's one that stands out as an all-time favorite. It's a regular source of nourishment: "What We Talk About When We Talk About Love" by Raymond Carver.

Maybe it's the old romantic in me. I'm not sure. I mean, the way Carver deals with powerful feelings and complex human desires, the way he helps us understand them, talks about them honestly; the way he writes them down, thinks them through, his economy of observation, his brevity and plain-talking. In everything he wrote, Carver never gave definitive answers. Most of his stories don't have storylines. Their endings trail off, usually poignantly. And yet, they're soaring acts of inventiveness, leaving us with a quiet and gracious sense of hope.

Carver acknowledged his debt to short story masters Anton Chekhov and Isaac Babel, even if his war stories and survivor tales bed themselves down in more mundane terrain: not so much the ruined tedium of the provincial Russian estate as workaday small-town America. Carver was an unassuming chronicler of the flawed lives of ordinary people, their struggles and yearnings, *our* struggles and yearnings. He never wrote epic tomes nor tackled grand historical themes.

"What We Talk About When We Talk About Love" is probably his best-known story. Published in 1981, it quickly knocked people out, knocking me out a decade later when I stumbled upon it as a graduate student in Baltimore. By then it was an American classic and Carver a martyred legend. Its setting is typically stripped down, typically centering on sharp dialogue and booze. Carver finally beat the bottle in the early 1980s, got remarried (to poet Tess Gallagher), found contentment, recognition, autumnal happiness, love—only to have lung cancer strike, seeing him off in 1988, aged fifty. "And did you get what / you wanted from this life, even so?" Carver wrote in a final poem, "Late Fragment." "I did / And what did you want? /... to feel myself / beloved on the earth."

Carver's own title for "What We Talk About When We Talk About Love" was "Beginners." But his longtime editor, Gordon Lish, hacked fifty percent off and renamed it. The Lish label stuck. Carver, appalled at first, wanted to pull his story but then had a change of heart and kept Lish's honed version. Lish hacked away at many other Carver stories over the years, stripping them down to bare chicken bones. After Carver's death, Tess Gallagher republished her late husband's restored takes, bundling them together under the banner *Beginners*, letting readers finally glimpse Carver at full length and full speed. It's a hit-and-miss affair. Sometimes the longer versions are richer than Lish's edited ones. Other times Lish's edits seem right.

"What We Talk About When We Talk About Love" sees two couples—Mel and Terri, and Nick and Laura—drink gin around a kitchen table. They get on to the subject of love, its nature, what it means to each of them, what it once meant. As evening sets in, and the room dims, they get progressively drunker, more maudlin. What we hear is intense talk, a memorable encounter deeper and more probing, maybe even more disturbing, than any Platonic symposium. "The kind of love I'm talking about," says Mel, "is love where you don't try to kill people." "What do any of us really know above love," he says. "It seems to me we're just beginners at love." "There was a time when I loved my first wife more than life itself. But now I hate her guts. I do. How do you explain that?"

Terri says Mel is into spiritual love. Terri once dated a guy called Ed who loved her yet *did* try to kill her. "We lived like fugitives," Terri says. Until Ed killed himself. He drank rat poison but lived. His teeth pulled away from his gums and stuck out like fangs afterward. Then he shot himself. His head swelled up to twice its normal size and he died two days later. "I just wouldn't call Ed's behavior love. That's all I'm saying, honey," says Mel. "It was love," Terri says. "Sure, it's abnormal in most people's eyes. But he was willing to die for it. He did die for it."

"What about you guys?" wonders Terri, questioning Laura and Nick. "Does that sound like love to you?" Nick isn't sure; he seems more realist than romantic. "I'm the wrong person to ask," he says. "I didn't even know the man. I've only heard his name mentioned in passing. I wouldn't know. You'd have to know the particulars. But I think what you're saying is that love is an absolute." "You know the kind of love I'm talking about," Mel says. "Physical love, that impulse that drives you to someone special, as well as love of the other person's being, his or her essence, as it were. Carnal love and, well, call it sentimental love, the day-to-day caring about the other person."

The gins flows. "A toast to love. To true love," Mel cries, raising his empty glass. "Honey, I'm just talking," he says. "All right? I don't have to be drunk to say what I think. I mean, we're all just talking, right?" They lose the sun; twilight encroaches. "I could hear my heart beating," Carver has Nick muse. "I could hear everyone's heart. I could hear the human noise we sat there making, not one of us moving, not even when the room went dark."

For a while I've dreamed of putting this story to work, making it work where my heart beats, in my world. I've wondered if I could ever write something using Carver as a loose guide, his story as a sort of template, dialoging about what we mean when we talk about cities, what cities have meant to me, meant to others. Urban studies is something I've talked and written a lot about for decades. That's been my world, my universe. But I'd like to try to give the conversation a different spin, another voice, another idiom. I'd love to talk about cities and love.

What are we talking about when we talk about cities? Do we need to know the particulars, the details? Can we talk about cities in the absolute, get at their essence, beneath the particulars? Is it possible to love a city? To hate a city? Can we talk about cities in a carnal sense? Sentimentally? Can we urbanists toast true love? Does true love last? Might we fall out of love with a city? Might we find true love *in* the city? I'd always wanted to talk about romantic love and the city but wasn't sure how.

In a strange way, though, I'd already seen "What We Talk About When We Talk About Love" find an urban staging: through the dark drama of a fascinating film, *Birdman*. Alejandro G. Iñárritu's 2014 Oscar winner moves inside and beyond Carver's story, doing so in New York, starring Michael Keaton as a washed up Riggan Thomson. Twenty-years back, Riggan was the Hollywood action hero Birdman. Now, flabbier, aged, more desperate, he's directing, acting, and partially bankrolling a Broadway production of Carver's classic story. He's out to reclaim artistic integrity, or else affirm it for the first time, to rejuvenate a flagging career as well as a failing marriage. His relationship with his daughter is fraught.

The critics are out to slam him. He's on the psychological edge, staring into a deep abyss, yearning to fly high again.

Riggan might be famous yet he's still an authentic Carver cast-off, hardly sleeping, twitchy, tormented by an inner Birdman voice, his Freudian alter-ego. Sixty is the new forty this voice tells him; go and show those wimpy fuckers what Birdman can do. Everything's on the line, including Riggan's own life. In one scene, a co-star reminds him that Carver put his liver into his stories. So what's Riggan's problem? On stage, Riggan plays Mel as well as the psychotic Ed. In the play's climax he ups the ante with a real gun, and live ammunition, and blows his nose off.

Carver's spirit is there in *Birdman*. So is New York's. New York is part of the drama, both subject and object, its cast and staging. We follow a handheld camera tracking Riggan as he navigates the worn inner sanctum of the St. James Theatre. We feel, close-up, its grungy narrow backstage corridors, its peeling wallpaper, its frayedness. (The theater is old, built in 1927.) The shabbiness gets under your skin. It reeks of the Big Apple. We can smell New York here, *feel* the city's odor invade our senses, enter us, as we watch. We can see through Riggan's eyes, too, witness how—once the spotlight is off, once the actors start playing themselves—the glamor becomes depressingly unglamorous. New York's romance is a grimy anti-romance.

New York is there when Riggan pushes open the theater's side door, letting him and Carver flood onto 44th Street, into the neon nighttime. Midtown skyscrapers leap out in front of us. We can hear the car horns, the police sirens, watch the rush of people, listen to their loud chatter, to the crazies howling. In a hilarious scene, Riggan has a smoke break between acts. He's standing outside in his dressing gown, agitated and fidgety. Suddenly, a stagehand shuts the side door behind him. He's locked out. His robe is jammed in the door. He can't rip it free. He has to take it off and, in only his underwear, streak through a Times Square that brims with crowds.

In its radiant glow, he legs it around to the theater's main entrance. He looks like the chicken with leukemia he said he was. He's quickly spotted, recognized, videoed. Within minutes his bizarre image has been tweeted thousands of times. He's the talk of the town. Then he bursts into the auditorium, running through the audience, following the footlights, bearing his gun, a real one. Now he's Ed. The audience sits there aghast, perplexed and terrified at the realism, at the sight of a desperate Ed played by a desperate Riggan performing a desperate Carver. They love him. Riggan is learning how to talk about love, authentic love.

Carver had a hero and role model: Chekhov. After Carver died, many obituaries suggested Carver was "America's Chekhov." The accolade would have likely thrilled, if embarrassed, the humble Carver. He loved Chekhov, even inserted some of the Russian's poems into his own book of poems, never claiming they were his own, merely happy to see Chekhov there beside him, in print. Carver said, "Chekhov is the greatest short story writer who ever lived." "Anyone who reads literature," said Carver, "anyone who believes, as one must, in the transcendent power of art, sooner or later has to read Chekhov." Tess Gallagher wrote how "Ray had somehow won permission through a lifetime of admiration [of Chekhov] to take up his work with the audacity of love."

What would Carver have thought of one rendering of his beloved Chekhov, done not far away from the drama of *Birdman*, just around the corner on 42nd Street? When French director Louis Malle decided to film André Gregory's stage production of Chekhov's *Uncle Vanya*, calling it *Vanya on 42nd Street*, Carver had been dead for six years. Carver never saw how boredom and dissatisfaction in *fin-de-siècle* rural Russia got a distinctively New York makeover, a vividly urban readaptation of his hero's classic. Not least because of its venue: a space once housing the raunchy Ziegfeld Follies, the dilapidated art nouveau New Amsterdam Theatre, built in 1903, a few years after Chekhov's play premiered.

For much of the 1980s, André Gregory rehearsed Chekhov nearby in another boarded up Broadway jewel, the ruined Victory Theater. There he persuaded a small group of actors—Julianne Moore and playwright Wallace Shawn included—to show up for free, in their spare time, to rehearse *Uncle Vanya* each week, for years, a marathon odyssey before a handful of invited friends and family. Gregory later managed to raise $900,000 to fund and entice Louis Malle to shoot the entire play. (Malle had worked with Gregory and Shawn before, on the 1982 miracle *My Dinner With André*.)

They spent two weeks filming in the New Amsterdam Theatre, in a movie that begins with footage of the actors playing themselves, dressed in everyday modern garb, emerging from the subway. They greet one another, pace through Times Square's streets to the theater. Their faces bob along with other faces bobbing along in the glorious jam that is midtown Manhattan, soundtracked by Joshua Redman's jazz groove, "Chill." Moments later, Gregory and Shawn stand alongside a food vendor. They talk to one another near the New Amsterdam's lobby, munching, in the cool spring air, on a pre-performance knish.

The New Amsterdam closed its doors in 1982, leaving rats to gnaw away at a lot of it. Yet Gregory and Malle stole a little corner of the stage, in this crumbling beauty, to create beautiful crumbling art, Chekhov in the city. Gregory himself is something of a maestro of ruins. He's directed many plays in ruined theaters, ruined castles, ruined men's clubs, ruined riding stables. Why so many ruins, he once wondered? Probably because he's a director allergic to formal theaters.

Gregory recalls an old German theater director once coming to a rehearsal. He loved the ruined space, thought it truly wonderful. Gregory asked what, specifically, he found so wonderful. "How perfect," the old director said. "This ruin of a theater, on this ruin of a street, in this ruin of a culture, in this ruin of a nation, and here inside the ruin on a stage, this peculiar little group of actors who still care about culture and art, who still care about *Vanya*—just imagine—and watching them, this peculiar tiny little audience who also cares, and behind them in the vast empty auditorium, the ghosts of thousands of audience members who in the past did something like this every night."

Malle's camera rolls in the ruins. On film, the actors make ready for their performance. They casually chat to each other. They complain of being tired. They pour tea, set up the table, arrange the bench, organize the chairs, the sofa. "Drink?" actor Phoebe Brand asks Larry Pine, who plays Doctor Astrov. "No. No thank you," Pine replies. "I don't want it somehow." "A little Vodka?" wonders Brand. "Not today," says Pine. "How long have we known each other?" Pine enquires. "How long," Brand says, "Lord, let me see…Eleven years. More." "How much have I changed?" Pine asks. "Very much I think," says Brand, "your looks have faded." "Ah," Pine laments, "I have become a different man."

Then, all of a sudden, the camera shifts. Now we can see what Brand and Pine were seeing: a tiny audience in front of them, with André Gregory in the front row. He's smiling like the Cheshire Cat. We've been watching Chekhov for a while; the play had already begun, even before we'd realized it. Doctor Astrov and Marina were dialoging the opening of act 1, in a brilliantly seamless shift between the street and stage, between modern life and modern art. Gregory said this "was what it feels like to live a life"—not just to perform a life. There's something marvelously urban about this, too. We can sense a great bustling metropolis somewhere nearby, somehow *inside* the drama, part of the drama, there for us to try to comprehend.

Doctor Astrov is bored with life, hates his "provincial life," he says, hates "his Russian life," "with all the power of my soul." The only glimmer of light before him is his one passion: his forest. "I hear the forest sighing," he says. "I *planted* that forest…I watch it take root, it grows, it sways in the wind, and I feel such pride." And yet as Astrov talks about thrills of nature in the ruins of urban nature, urban nature sneaks into the frame: in the muffled distance, we hear the hum of cars, the honking of horns, the blaring of a fire truck, even the rumbling of a subway car beneath the earth. "Tell us something *new*," Astrov asks Vanya. "Something new, what's new? Nothing's changed," Vanya says, "I'm the same…no, probably worse, for I have grown lazy and complain all day. What's changed…?" It's a troubling question. No city person could ever ask it. What's changed? Everything's changed, is changing; Times Square was changing, quite literally then as Astrov and Vanya spoke. New York was changing, all cities change; there's always something new going on.

Years ago I read a great book about Times Square, reveling in everything Vanya's life lacked: FASCINATION. FASCINATION was a winking sign in Times Square that lured novelist John Rechy into his city of night. Indeed, *City of Night*, from 1963, spoke a lot about the city, about Times Square, about how Rechy surrendered to its world: "I stand on 42nd Street and Broadway looking at the sign flashing news from the Times Tower…The world is losing. The hurricane still menaces…I feel explosively excited to be on this street—at the sight of the people and lights, sensing the anarchy…like a possessive lover—or like a powerful drug—it lured me. FASCINATION! I returned, dazzled, to this street. The giant sign winked its welcome:

F*A*S*C*I*N*A*T*I*O*N.

Rechy was yet another Carver cast-off, a furtive underground man, a lonesome exile and gay hustler. He found dangerous comfort and companionship in Times Square, a special public space for adult encounter and sexual intrigue. Home of the Ziegfeld Follies and Tin Pan Alley, vaudeville and burlesque, risqué and "legit" theater, peep and porn shows, drug pushers and hipsters, since 1905 Times Square's neon light has shone radiantly while casting long dark shadows. It has satisfied an array of appetites and fantasies, challenged norms about public morality and individual behavior, about private parts in public places, and entered into the popular psyche of Americans and New Yorkers alike.

FASCINATION set its tone. But what kind of fascination? When we talk about the fascination of cities, it seems the fascination of having people around, lots of people, day and night, ordinary people, different people, unusual people, weird people. Cities are arenas that accept weirdness, that let weirdness coexist with ordinariness. Cities are special environments where the social and the physical come together, where fascination means a certain intensity, a certain drunkenness.

Yet when we talk about cities we aren't only talking about fascination; we're also talking about *ambivalence*. In the twenty-odd years since *Vanya on 42nd Street*, the New Amsterdam Theatre has been gleamingly renovated by Disney. They've orchestrated a massive cleansing of the district. The winking sign across the Square today is the $20 million NASDAQ sign, giving up-to-the-second stock prices of hundreds of high-tech companies, projecting two ads a minute. Nearby are billboards as big as buildings, exhibiting beautiful corporate bodies, promoting Gap, L'Oréal, Liz Claiborne, Tommy Hilfiger. FASCINATION is the fascination of media conglomerates Condé Nast, Reuters, MTV, Bertelsmann, and Virgin. Lonely underground men, once starved for love, have given way to rich overground executives who manufacture love.

Somebody who understood the ambivalence of the modern city, and the ambivalence of modern love, maybe better than anybody, was the New York urbanist Marshall Berman. His book *On the Town* was both a love letter to and lover's spat over Times Square. When Marshall spoke about cities here was a guy worth listening to and talking with. In the 1980s, when I was a student in the UK, I fell in love with his great book on modernity, *All That Is Solid Melts into Air*, from 1982. In the 1990s, I fell in love with Marshall himself, moved to New York, got to know him as a friend, talked a lot with him, admired him, learned from him, quit New York, fell out with him. Then he died, before we'd really made up.

In his Times Square book, Marshall talks about his subject matter like Socrates talked about ancient Athens. His viewpoint is skeptical yet loving, questioning yet appreciative, critical yet rarely damning. We might say that when Marshall talked about cities he talked *dialectically* about cities. And he knew all about Carveresque compassion as well, which made his cultural criticism approachable and original. Here's a bit of his spiel on Times Square: "The big new buildings are more overbearing than the ones they replaced, but none of them is anywhere near as bad as the really dreadful skyscrapers that blasted into the Square's heart a generation ago." "When I think of the appalling level of big buildings erected in New York in my lifetime," Marshall said, "the mediocrity of the new Times Square looks like progress."

Like many who remember old Times Square, Marshall felt tired of all the different colored uniforms that now patrol the theater district, the city cops with machine guns and body armor, the corporate security guards, the private task forces—the NYSD, UDC, BID, and many more. He felt menaced by them, flooded out by them. Still, "I'm old enough to remember," he reflected, "when you couldn't find any uniforms at all. One twilight evening on the deuce in April 1980, I saw a man crack another man's skull with a club that looked like a prop from *The Flintstones*. The man went out like a light and spurted blood all over the street, from which everyone instantly disappeared. I yelled '*Help!*' and found myself totally alone. I couldn't find a cop, no one in any nearby shop would let me call one, and the guy just kept bleeding. I'll take the uniforms, thanks, so long as they know how to keep people on the street alive."

Later, in *On the Town* (in its epilogue "Reuters and Me," a wink to Michael Moore's *Roger & Me*) another "fat man" finds himself threatened by a security guard, this time outside the Reuters building at 3 Times Square. Marshall himself is standing around one humid summer's afternoon, taking notes for his book, sketching the people and signs around him, in his shorts and T-shirt, when a security guard told him he wasn't allowed to stand in front of the building. Taken aback, *What*? Marshall exclaimed. There were other guys around, in fancy suits, standing and talking. What about them? They're not shooed away? If he didn't leave, the guard warned, he'd be "forcibly removed." "Why did I let myself get moved on?" Marshall asked himself afterward. "Why didn't I stand up for my rights," his *right to the city*, ordinary people's right? "I felt terrible, still feel terrible, that I just let it be."

In the early 1990s, Marshall told me he was working on a book called "*Living for the City*—after the Stevie Wonder song." He'd been thinking about this book for a long while, ever since finishing *All That is Solid Melts into Air*. The problem was he hadn't written much of it—hadn't been able to, was paralyzed somehow, blocked. He'd continued to talk and teach, in Harlem, at the City College of New York (CCNY), and at the City University of New York (CUNY) Graduate Center, and plenty poured out of him—essays and reviews in publications like *The Nation, The Village Voice,* and *Dissent.* But all that looked like a pile of fragments, he said.

Living for the city had been rough during the 1980s, rougher than talking about it. Marshall's town, New York, was blighted by fiscal crisis, deindustrialization, decline, and hard drugs, even while banks and Wall Street piled up spectacular profits. It was a bonfire of the vanities that Mayor Ed Koch ran with aggressive bluster and meanness. "It felt as if he poisoned the air every time he opened his mouth," Marshall said. The decade started off personally very badly, too. In 1980, Marshall's five-year-old son, Marc, died. Then Marshall got sick himself, nearly dying of a brain abscess.

I remember we were sitting across from one another in a booth at one of Marshall's favorite eateries, the Metro Diner, on Broadway at West 100th Street, on the Upper West Side. The Metro has been around since 1989. But the site itself is one of the neighborhood's oldest structures, dating back to 1871, when it was a grocery store. Its owner today is a Greek-immigrant businessman, Fanis Tsiamtsiouris, known as "Frank." Seven hundred cups of coffee get poured there each day, a hundred and fifty-odd hamburgers grilled, and twelve hundred eggs cracked open by staff hailing from all over the world.

I sat overlooking 100th Street, looking westward, on the lookout for Marshall. But he came from the other direction, from the subway. When he arrived he said I should shift around to face the other way, to look eastward. He was keen for me to watch the action along Upper Broadway, the neighborhood's central artery. Upper Broadway was very special to him and he wanted to share the pleasure. He wanted me to see it for myself. It was such a sweet thing to do. I'll always remember it. The Metro Diner had been one of my first New York ports of call with Marshall. Unbeknownst to me then, two decades later, it would be his last. He'd keel over in the morning on that awful New York day, September 11th, in 2013, his heart giving out, breakfasting with his old Bronx pal, the photographer Mel Rosenthal. Marshall was seventy-two.

After our Metro Diner encounter, Marshall invited me back to his apartment. I schlepped slowly around the corner with him, up the gentle incline of West 100th Street, past the Ansche Chesed Synagogue he sometimes attended, and the Morningside Montessori school his son Danny would go to, then right on

West End Avenue, to a building older than most of the neighborhood's, constructed in 1913, after George and Edward Blum's Art Nouveau design, frayed by years but still with its strikingly ornate façade.

The first thing that hit anybody entering Marshall's seventh-floor apartment was *books*. Copies and assorted translations of *All That Is Solid* were stacked overhead in the coat closet; novels filled shelves in the main passage way; a hidden revolving bookshelf contained a voluminous Marx and Freud collection, "needing security clearance for access," he'd joke. Books burst out of the cupboards, lined the walls of an adjoining room, where, in a little niche in the far corner, adjacent to a window, peering down onto the street, lurked Marshall's work desk, his intellectual cockpit.

Marshall took off his shoes and socks and encouraged me to hang out with him on the living room floor, next to the sofa, not on it. Soon his curious mind was gently pumping me full with questions: who was I? What did I love? Whom did I love? It was our own secret be-in. I was thrilled. I'd read him for years; now, I was slouching next to him on the rug, in his world! It was a newfound land for me. And I wanted more of it. This was the life I wanted to lead, the city life I wanted, the way I wanted to *be* in the city, in New York, on the Upper West Side. You know, an apartment full of books and art, tall ceilings, diners close-by, a bagel for breakfast. Nothing spick-and-span; a little shabby, a little *ruined*—a life burning in every moment.

Not long afterward, I found this city life, made it to New York, to the Upper West Side, got myself a Green Card, was a permanent resident. Great floodgates of the wonder-world swung open. It had been Marshall who'd inspired me to come. And I did for a while, for several troubled years, happy years. Marshall and wife Shellie became dear friends, a dynamic duo inspiring my wife and I, inspiring us how to live, how to be happy, in love. Marshall wrote us a glowing co-op board reference, helping us buy ourselves a broom closet on West 93rd Street, near Central Park, telling them how much we loved the Upper West Side, how much the Upper West Side needed people who cared, people like us. So please let them into your building! That was pretty much it for Marshall, his style, both lyrical and childlike, a truth and sincerity that cut through the crap, that made crap honest. My love affair with the city had begun, had found vital human expression. But like all true love it was impulsive, as crazy as Carver's Ed's, never running smooth.

I did fall in love with New York City. Not exactly at first sight. It was something else. I mean, I was too young then to know true love—apart from for my mother. It was 1970. I was only ten. My parents took me to visit my Aunt Rene, my mother's sister, who, since 1968, had lived near Boston. We spent a few days exploring New York beforehand, staying in some fleapit hotel near Times Square. To make the trip over, my mum and dad saved money for ages, forsaking a lot. My pals at school couldn't believe I was going to America, especially because they had parents much richer than mine.

For years afterward I kept the free Pan Am bag we'd received onboard the plane. In it, I stashed the floor plan of the Empire State Building that I'd collected. I had big ideas about living in the Empire State Building, not knowing, nor caring, that nobody actually lived in the Empire State Building. Atop of the world, on its eighty-sixth floor, I'd seen before me my own destiny, down there, on the street, with its crowds, its yellow phantasmagoria. That was what *I* wanted to talk about, this adventure urbanism. It was more intrigue than love, more fascination, piqued by fear. This was a scary place for a kid from Liverpool whose farthest voyage hitherto had been to a crummy beach in North Wales, where it rained all the while.

Alien smells, weird names, heat, people—most of all I remember *people*—even more than tall buildings, people on the street, people just standing about, people doing nothing in the midst of other people, waiting on street corners; and litter, swirling mounds of litter everywhere, getting tossed in the warm breeze; and cabs and car horns honking. Everything seemed in motion, in technicolor. The frame was full; stuff was happening. In Liverpool, the frame was empty, lifeless, life-sapping. Everything was gray, different shades of gray; darker grays for the buildings, lighter grays for the sky. Sometimes it was the other way around. The gray in gray of life grown old, even while I was young. Grayness entered your soul. I wanted color, life. I wanted *elsewhere.*

Years later, I oddly grew proud to have come from Liverpool, felt much more Liverpudlian than British, felt like I came from a city rather than a country. Yet growing up in Liverpool then, becoming an adolescent *in* Liverpool, I hated the place with all the power of my soul. I think I felt someone had stolen my youth there, that I was missing out on something, that I watched my childhood dissipate into damp Liverpool air. Somehow it was the city's fault. My parents were both loving; they did their best. It wasn't anything to do with them, this feeling.

At sixteen, I quit school. Or maybe school quit me. I entered adulthood to seek my misfortune. I did miserably at my exams, failed almost everything, had little choice but to wander into a series of dull, pointless, and senseless jobs that most people thought I was lucky to get. I was a clerk in a pension company, in an insurance company, at the dock board, at a shipping firm. I busked tables in a fast food restaurant, worked a broiler at a steak house, did landscaping, was a maître d' at a nightclub, an assistant at a sports store, a dole office clerk, a police fingerprint clerk, a junior at the nuclear power monitoring board. Always and everywhere at the very bottom of the rung, a veritable dog's body who made the tea and ran the errands. And every time I got fired.

It was just as well I hadn't read Isaac Babel in those days, that other Carver hero; I'd have been even more depressed, for being such a wimp. I hadn't yet heard Babel say: "*I refused to become a clerk*." I thought this a beautiful declaration. But I hadn't, couldn't, follow it back then. I didn't have the intelligence to follow it. "Better to suffer hunger, prison, and homelessness," Babel said, "than sit at a clerk's desk ten hours a day." I couldn't have agreed more. "We have been born to delight in labor, fighting, and love," Babel said. "There is no particular daring in making such a pledge, but I haven't broken it to this day, nor will I."

For ten years—my lost decade—I did these ridiculous, deadening tasks. I read later that Raymond Carver did all sorts of dead-end jobs, too, and that made me feel less bad. He'd worked in a sawmill, as a janitor, a deliveryman, a gas station attendant, and stockroom boy. But there was a difference between him and me. He was a struggling writer with justifiable ambitions about going up in the world, becoming a famous writer. I was a struggling nobody, with no qualifications and no prospects, no nothing, going no place. I thought this was it, till I got a lucky break to go back to school, to get a college degree.

Where Liverpool and me came unstuck was when my mother died. I held the city responsible. Can you hold a city responsible for a death? My mother was dying of lung cancer in a hospital called "The Royal," a massive, God-ugly hellhole near Liverpool's city center. It had been a bright sparked idea in the 1980s to close down all the smaller "inefficient" hospitals, the handy local hospitals, and amalgamate them into single, giant, centralized structures, unwieldy alienating behemoths. (It's scheduled to become an even bigger, unwieldy alienating behemoth; the Royal's latest reincarnation is due to be unveiled later in 2018.) It'd make things better and cheaper, they said then, and still say, when it only makes services worse and more costly. And as those little old hospitals got demolished, their land was sold off for a song. Many today, like the one I was born in, along Smithdown Road, are giant supermarkets.

She was at home the day she took a turn for the worse. The ambulance came for her in the afternoon. She looked very bad. I knew she'd not long left. She couldn't move. It took two ambulance guys to haul her onto a bed. Then she had some kind of seizure and I thought she was going right in front of me. Her eyes disappeared around the back of her head and she wasn't responding to questions. They gave her oxygen and before long she came back around, conscious again. I went with her in the ambulance. Everything was shaking around as the vehicle raced on. Every jerk and vibration added to her distress, every pothole and bump, every bit of crappy, neglected road we went along became a form of torture for her, and for me. I remember cursing the council and the government and all those politicians and the rich—everyone responsible or irresponsible. I cursed the lot.

She was checked in at hospital. Soon my dad and I tried to find out where she was. What was happening? She was in the lobby waiting for a ward, a curtain pulled around her bed. A doctor was coming, we were told. When was the doctor coming? The nurses didn't know. The doctor was "coming down," always coming down. My mother was in pain everywhere. I went in search of somebody to help. But nobody could help. Nobody was around. I felt like screaming. Eventually somebody did come to take her away, for x rays and blood tests. The porter wheeled her out. We followed. She was left in a corridor outside the x-ray unit. Over half an hour passed. If we hadn't been there, she would have been abandoned, all alone in a desolate passageway, neglected and seemingly forgotten. There she was, tucked up in her bed, head peeking out, skull-like already; a bit of wiry, ruffled gray hair stuck up from it.

Finally, they took her away. We were left waiting. Waiting in the waiting room. It backed on to the out-patient emergency. A group of four or five kids sat round, fourteen or fifteen year olds, one with his arm in a sling. Tough kids—scallies, you'd call them in Liverpool—laughing and joking around, making noise. One was smoking a cigarette despite large signs announcing this was forbidden. Put it out, I told him. Nobody else dared tell them. People had become immune to, or too fearful of, scumbags to say anything. He made a wisecrack: they changed the rules yesterday; you can smoke now. "Quit it," I said, "*put the fucker out*!" My dad said something, too, and they started on him. The lad did finally extinguish the thing. I think he could tell I meant business, that I *did* want trouble. I was so distraught, enraged, that I had no fear of pain or injury, nor death. I wanted to beat their heads to a pulp. I was desperate and they knew it. I could smell their anxiety, their fear, as I prowled menacingly near them. I'd out-Liverpooled them. It was that pathetic.

The ward she was taken to said it all: "ACUTE ADMISSIONS," Ward 3a. Actually, she had a tiny room to herself. Bare, quiet, deathly, devoid of anything human or personal. A box of nothingness. Sixty-eight years. "Is man no more than this?" The end came next day: May 14, 1996.

By then I hadn't lived in Liverpool for several years. After my mother's death, I said I'd never come back, not ever. That was it for me, *finito*, between me and it—my native city. I'd moved to London, landed a teaching job at a university. I never liked the job much. I've never liked any job much. Academia wasn't for me. But it was the nearest I could come to having a job that wasn't a real job. When it started to become a real job, I knew it was time to get out. But that came later.

In those days I rented a studio apartment, a tiny single room, off Russell Square. I could stroll to work, down Southampton Row and Kingsway, dodging traffic, risking life and limb, across Aldwych, over onto the Strand. Central London became my little village, my urban laboratory. I'd not venture much beyond Soho to the west, Clerkenwell to the east, Hampstead to the north, and Festival Hall to the south, going everywhere on foot. The Underground slowed me down.

This zone sustained my urban needs for a while. I had a bookstore nearby—Judd Books, a favorite—a few cafés, and an arts cinema practically next door. My building was a darkly noir 1930s structure, a surreal place. Inside it looked like something out of *Barton Fink*, right down to the moldy, peeling wallpaper. There were scores of long, eerily empty corridors, all with the same faded maroon carpet, looking as if it'd been there since the very beginning, bearing the initials "RC." Along each corridor were lots of uniform doors, behind which, you knew, lay single rooms, tiny rooms, secret lives. But you never saw a soul. There were hundreds of people here, yet nobody ever about.

I had a sofa bed. Unfolded, it took up almost the entire floorspace. To begin with, I tried sleeping on it. But the big problem was *noise*, coming from above, drowning out even the traffic din outside, the black cabs cruising up and down Woburn Place. Throughout the *whole* night, through the flimsy, paper-thin ceiling, I could hear a TV, and what seemed to be a young woman giggling, presumably at the TV. She was an addicted watcher, having great fun. For a few weeks it drove me crazy. I went around half-dazed, bleary-eyed. I needed to take action so decided to get myself a sleeping bag and camping mat.

I'd bivouac along the apartment's narrow corridor, just about long enough, and wide enough, to let me be quietly prostrate. Relief! Now, I could camp out, and sleep, in relative peace, doing so like this for a year. Until I moved out across the street, right across the street, to another apartment, buying—when you could still afford to buy—a bigger studio on Coram Street. I carried my modest possessions—a few boxes of books, my sleeping bag and camping mat, a suitcase of old clothes—single-handedly, taking a half hour to move out and move in to my new abode, a week after my mother's death. She never did see my new home. That's probably why it never felt like home.

The café around the corner, on Marchmont Street, served as an extension of my living room. I'd sit there for hours when I could, when I wasn't teaching, during vacation times, drinking coffee, thinking about stuff, losing myself, trying to find myself, all the while watching the world go by outside. I liked that. I felt a part of the action; detached from it, anonymous, sufficiently absent, yet absolutely *present.* I was still yet still moving. I was here and there and everywhere.

Sometimes I thought about Marshall in New York, and about the Metro Diner. Then New York felt closer, somehow more imaginable. I was living it vicariously, from a perch right next to the window, high up on a stool. I surveyed the crossroads, at the junction with Tavistock Place, eyeing things to the west and east, everything to the north; and, if I turned around, I could glimpse the street to the south as well. I could see it all, from this ordinary little patch on planet Earth. Sometimes, while I sat, I thought I didn't have to go out into the world at all, because, here, the world sort of came to me.

I drank cappuccino and ate the same thing each time I was there. Before long, the proprietors—two gruff Egyptian brothers—knew what I wanted, were already preparing it as I entered: chicken avocado on a bagel; a white chocolate slice came afterward. I'd sip my cappuccino, stare out the window, listen to the radio, feel the pulse of neighborhood life going about its daily business. I was supposed to be writing a book about the city, about different cities, from a theoretical standpoint. The thing was that the city—London—got in the way, blocked my path. The living city somehow intervened in the theoretical city. The more I tried to capture its mood and structure, its people and flow, its mysteries, the more it eluded my grasp. The words, especially those wooden academic words, never seemed quite right. There were two different worlds at play, two different pictures: the realm of experience and something behind that experience, beyond that experience, the context which makes that experience possible. Those pictures complemented each other, I knew, but I wasn't sure how I could bring each of them together.

One picture was right in front of my nose, before my gaze, outside the window ahead. It was a fish store the other side of the street, on the northeast corner of Marchmont Street. The store still had its original green tiling on the outside wall, Deco tiling from the 1930s. I bought fish sometimes from this store. Yet now there's a large sign, "UNDER OFFER," emblazoned on its window, looming ominously.

Last time I was there I'd asked the owner what was going on. He told me the lease was coming up for renewal. He couldn't afford the new rate, couldn't renew it on what he takes in every year. The supermarket in the Brunswick Centre sells fish now. He can't compete. And, besides, as the older population dies off, fewer people, he said, seem to want to cook fish anymore. He hardly makes ends meet. It's not worth him staying. So he's selling up. Soon it'll be a photographic store, serving the tourists from the hotels around the corner. He says he's a bit embarrassed, wants to keep it hush-hush. He doesn't want fuss from the locals, just wants out fast, with as much money as he can grab. Difficult to blame him. But all this stuff about leases and economics is that other picture we can't see from our experience. It's that what we sometimes *need* to talk about when we talk about cities.

Over those months, I had the idea to write a different book, with a title that had been staring me in the face all along: *The Café on the Corner*. I'd simply write about what I saw each day looking out of the window, write about what I felt while I was looking, trying to understand these feelings. I wrote up copious notes, laid out plans, themes, possible chapter headings. Then I had a change of heart about the title, thought I'd call it something else: *The Café in the Implicate Order*. Nothing ever came of it. Neither title came off. It had something to do with my troubled state of mind, with my unsettledness, with the messy imprecision of feeling. I was grieving, it's clear now, yet had no one to talk to about it. It stirred up inside me. In high summer, drizzly November infused my soul.

When I wasn't sitting in the café on the corner, I would enter that implicate order, wander in it; principally I'd wander, in the chaos outside. I'd seek out refuge in the busiest parts of town, amid crowds of people, usually around the British Museum; and then in the labyrinths of Soho, engaging in my daily *dérive*, often wandering at night, usually not even aware of where I was wandering to. It didn't matter where I went anyway. I didn't care. I just wanted to walk things off. I couldn't bear to stay at home, within my narrow four walls.

Out on the street my mind was someplace else, thinking about someplace else, though where, exactly, I no longer knew. I drifted between buildings, inanimate objects, in a somnolent daze. They spoke to me in a dismal language only I could hear. They asked only questions; never supplied answers. I walked for miles and miles, communing with darkened corners and quiet alleyways, with narrow streets—with ghosts. They guarded me somehow.

I traveled onward, toward a vast building. Taxis and people ahead. The vast building appeared. Tourists mobbed the sidewalk;

cameras, smiles, Japanese, Italians, Americans, more Japanese. I was sandwiched amongst them, constricted by them, a vise squeezing the breath out of me. I wanted to fly upward, sail overhead into the clouds, above and beyond them, or burrow beneath the pavement, scuttle into the shadows, into the darkness, invisible, like a cockroach in lamplight. But I couldn't. I was lured, sucked into their vortex, a bizarre source of comfort.

That idea of the *Café in the Implicate Order* was sparked by what literature I was reading and thinking about at the time. I was reading books on popular physics, and started to think and talk about cities the way quantum scientists like David Bohm talked and thought about subatomic reality, which was very, very small, not very, very big like a city. Yet it was more *how* these physicists thought about their subject matter, how they talked about their object. "The world appears as a complicated tissue of events," David Bohm said, "in which connections of different kinds alternate or overlap or combine and thereby determine the texture of the whole." The implicate order was this whole, "the ground from which reality emerges," an "unfolding order," he said.

Even in the chaos of the quantum world, where things behave weirdly inside the atom, where reality is both a wave and a particle, a flow and a static entity at the same time, there's also innate ordering and an implicit patterning. "By playing with both pictures," Bohm said, "by going from the one picture [wave] to the other [particle] and back again, we get the right impression of the strange kind of reality behind our experiments." I was a particle sat in my café with vast waves flowing outside. Together our cosmology was called the *urban*: whole cities made up of waves and particles, of leases flowing invisibly, of human entities visibly siting and walking around, colliding and interacting with each other, en masse. People mixed up with processes.

Cafés are part of this implicate order. In those days, cafés embodied my ideal of what cities should be; they still do. They're microcosms of a possible bigger microcosm. The greatest cafés have an atmosphere of democracy. I've always preferred them a bit down at heel, a bit downscale. Clientele can be as much poor and lonely as rich and idle with time on their hands. The menu isn't always great. Sometimes the food can be terrible. Everybody knows it. But the coffee is cheap and drinkable; the place is warm in winter, welcoming all seasons. Nobody is ever chased away.

In my ideal café, a writer-intellectual should be able to linger alongside the shabby and the broken, alongside regular workers, ordinary folk. I even think the writer-intellectual should have more in common with the shabby and the broken. They shouldn't be normal. What with sitting around on their own all day. At the café everybody can eat strawberry cheesecake together. Faithfuls who sit for a while, who show up most days, who express opinions, criticize the world and its politicians, gossip and grumble, read a newspaper, pen a few lines, talk and are willing to be talked to—all of them constitute what Isaac Bashevis Singer called the *cafeterianiks*.

Cafeterianiks, said Singer, usually have plenty of wrinkles, tell the same old stories and jokes, make the same old gestures. But it may happen, too, that they take out a scrap of paper from their pockets and read aloud a poem they've just written. In Singer's stories—stories Raymond Carver much admired—cafeterianiks are Eastern European immigrants, Jews and refugees who fled Hitler and find quiet comfort and unspoken camaraderie in New York's cafeterias, second homes when their first homes had been ransacked.

The cafeteria was a self-service affair. People lined up with trays, ate as much or as little as they wanted. Prices were cheap, frequenters poor. They privately schmoozed in public, purged their inner selves. "I like to take a tray with a tin knife, a fork, spoon and paper napkins," said one Singer character in "The Cafeteria," loosely modeled on Singer himself, "and choose at the counter the food I enjoy. Besides, I meet there the *landsleit* from Poland, as well as all kinds of literary beginners and readers who know Yiddish." Even after he won the Nobel Prize in 1978, even after he was famous and wealthy, vegetarian Singer still loved to eat rice pudding and stewed prunes in cheap New York cafeterias, many of which—like East Broadway's Garden Cafeteria, on the Lower East Side—are long gone. "The cafeteria closed. The neighborhood changed. Years passed... Yes, corpses walk on Broadway."

Raymond Carver's short story, "They're Not Your Husband," gives the cafeteria tale a little twist, viewing it from the standpoint of a woman, Doreen, who works the night shift in one. Doreen is a typically helpless Carver character. Equally typical is her uncanny ability to manage, to somehow get by, just about. Doreen lives in a trailer park with Earl, a small-time salesman currently between jobs. He goes to the state employment office once in a while. They've two kids. Doreen is on her feet all night, at a twenty-four-hour diner, pouring coffee, clearing away the plates, sending in the orders, bending up and down as men look at her ass.

She knows it. The men wink at each other at the counter when her skirt travels up her thighs. She has varicose veins and wants to lose a few pounds, but finds it hard. She doesn't like vegetables and can't afford steak. On the job, she picks at the food, can't help herself. Yet after a while she starts to lose weight; the pounds fall off. Soon she needs a smaller uniform. Her work colleagues say she's looking pale, a little too thin, is she okay? Husband Earl, a drinker, stops by at the diner sometimes, says she looks just fine;

tells them so. They're not your husband, he says. You don't have to live with them, he says. But I have to work with them, she says.

This sharp set-piece was brought to Hollywood by Robert Altman as part of *Short Cuts*, his epic three-hour retelling of nine Carver stories, "They're Not Your Husband," included; an idiosyncratic master director beds down an idiosyncratic master scribe in trashy suburban Southern Cal. Earl comes alive via Tom Waits, Doreen via Lily Tomlin, two nighthawks at the diner, in broad daylight.

In the 1950s, the Beats defined this terrain of the cafeterianik, made its banality literary. They cast neon-light on Dostoevsky and Nietzsche, blended low American culture and high European existentialism, Maxwell House with Thomas Mann, piecing them together, helping me understand diners and cafeterias after I'd first marvelled at them in 1970. There's an inspiring black and white image that I've always loved of Jack Kerouac, the most famous Beatster of all, in a cafeteria. Taken in 1959, on the Lower East Side, near an I.B. Singer hangout, Kerouac is sat at a booth with poets Allen Ginsberg and Gregory Corso, musician David Amram, and artist Larry Rivers.

The quartet had just appeared in Robert Frank's film *Pull My Daisy*, a twenty-eight minute miracle of the everyday city, scripted, with an ad-lib narration, by Kerouac himself. The film is an improvised alchemy that relives scenes from the ordinary madness of the life of Neal Cassady (Dean Moriarty in *On the Road*) with his wife Carolyn Robinson. Frank said *Pull My Daisy* "was made by non-professionals in search of that freer vision." Kerouac said of Frank, in his introduction to the photographer's masterpiece, *The Americans*, "You got eyes." I still remember why I loved *Pull My Daisy*: it was a snapshot of how I wanted to live, how I wanted to be in the city. Its impulse was a city of poets who were ordinary people and ordinary people who were poets, living in grungy affordability, a life that mixes the epic and the artistic with the everyday familial.

In that diner photo, Rivers seems to be doing the talking, relating some yarn or another. We can see Kerouac and Ginsberg gripped and grinning. A sidewall mirror reflects the counter and grill on the other side, with a plaque overhead, "BUTTERMILK." We can perhaps imagine Carver's Doreen waitressing there, serving all night long, worsening those varicose veins. On the table, there are cups of coffee, salt and pepper pots, a ketchup bottle, cigarette packets. The impression is youthful, happy and fraternal, full of promise for what lies ahead. But there's a presence of the moment, too, a *now*, of being there and only there—spontaneously captured by photographer John Cohen's lens. I remember feeling jealous: I have never been there like that. I wish I had.

I've another favorite cafeteria photo: one of our most famous urban talkers—Jane Jacobs—sitting at a booth, near the cheese-cake counter. It's the 1950s, around the time Kerouac and his buddies sat around a similar diner. Jane is there with two guys dressed in suits, talking shop, talking city, likely discussing an article she'd been commissioned to write for *Architectural Review*. She's scribbling something down in her notepad. The floor is checkered black and white lino, classic stuff, and there are coat stands at each booth.

Jacobs was a chip off Raymond Carver's block: She loved to tipple gin, made a mean "West Village Dry Martini," looked forward to it every night, often hastily making it amongst friends, pouring gin into glasses, adding an olive or pickled onion in each and a couple of drops of dry vermouth, a few ice cubes. She'd stir it with her forefinger. "You put your finger in it," she'd say, "and go swish, swish, swish…no time for niceties."

Around the table, the conversation between friends centered on that Carveresque theme of love: love of the city, love of the neighborhood, how to protect that love from people who hated it, from "official" people who thought that what you loved was a slum. As the gin flowed, the "Committee to Save the West Village" talked *city*. In the early 1960s, Manhattan's West Village had been designated a dump by city planners and government officials.

The data proved why. It was overcrowded, run down, an obstacle to progress. So, in February 1961, a month after the manuscript of Jane's book, *The Death and Life of Great American Cities*, had been submitted to Jason Epstein, her editor at Random House, the campaign to save the West Village was unleashed. Literary life became real life.

In *Death and Life*, Jacobs wrote lovingly and compellingly about our city streets, while fiercely denouncing the urban experts who towered over her. They saw nothing but statistics, people as abstractions, uprooted on the basis of mathematical averages. The larger the population abstraction and the greater the area to be cleared away, the easier it was to uproot. The experts weren't dealing with real people but with grains of sand and billiard balls, with rational "averages." Yet Jane wanted to "unaverage" things. With her catalogue of workaday street blocks, she offered another vision of the city that let ordinary citizens recognize themselves as city makers, not simply city users, and see their real place in urban life, perhaps for the first time.

She wrote without any credentials, critics said, without formal architectural or planning training, even without a university degree. And yet hers was a refreshing counter-narrative on the page, practiced out in public. When Robert Moses planned his huge swath through lower Manhattan, the multi-story Lower

Manhattan Expressway, razing vibrant communities in Greenwich Village and SoHo, Jacobs and her fellow residents mobilized to "KILL THE XPRESSWAY NOW!" She was arrested for inciting a riot. Moses decried his antagonists: "There's nobody against this—*nobody, nobody, nobody*. . .but a bunch of, a bunch of mothers!" At a hearing at the New York City Board of Estimate, Jacobs and fellow citizens ventured across the stage to get an audience with the bigwig professionals sitting above. "And this threw them into the most incredible tizzy," she recalled, "the idea of unarmed, perfectly gentle human beings just coming up and getting in close contact with them. You never saw people so frightened."

"There's no logic that can be superimposed on the city," Jacobs said. "People make the city, and it is to them, not buildings, that we must fit our plans." Professional experts must follow, must respond to ordinary citizens—not the other way around. "The citizen should be the ultimate expert," she argued. What's needed is something the expert so lacked: "an observant eye, curiosity about people, and a willingness to walk." "Let the citizens decide what end results they want," Jacobs said, "and they can adapt the rebuilding machinery to suit them. If new laws are needed, they can agitate to get them." "What a wonderful challenge there is! If this means leaving room for the incongruous, or the vulgar or the strange, that is part of the challenge, not the problem."

Hers wasn't only the kind of city I wanted to live in; this was a method of studying cities I also wanted to follow. I loved that it was low-budget, no-thrills, qualitative and subjective, earthy and commonsensical, based on somewhere nearby, somewhere out the window, somewhere with you in focus, part of the action. The experience of the city isn't reducible to a counting game, Jacobs said, to statistics and population densities, to something read off the census or "officially" mapped. There's a lot more going on, she revealed, a lot more *there* there. I knew then, as I sat in my café on the corner, why I had so much trouble writing about the city: It was hard to write about that there.

Those café days along Marchmont Street convinced me that Jane knew what she was talking about when she talked about cities. One thing she insisted upon was that cities need *hearts*. Can we hear that heart beating, the human noise it helps make? There's a natural anatomy of community hearts. Big cities usually have more than one heart. Yet always these hearts will beat at busy pedestrian intersections. "Wherever they develop spontaneously," Jacobs said, hearts "are almost invariably consequences of two or more intersecting streets, well used by pedestrians." They'll have corner stores or corner cafés, corner pubs or corner public squares. Hearts thrive off diversity, not homogeneity. City blocks need high-yield, middling-yield, low-yield, and no-yield enterprises. And yet, increasingly, it's high-yields only, making old fish stores pay up any way they can. Rich people see city hearts as profitable financial investments. In the mix there's eventually not much mix: prominent city hearts become functionally and financially standardized. Their blood runs thin. They need life support.

The summer after my mother's death I sat near Marchmont Street's heart, at the intersection of Sandwich and Leigh Streets, a quieter spot. I was there one evening with my father. He'd come down from Liverpool to stay with me. I took the floor, on my old camping mat and sleeping bag; he the futon I had permanently put down as a bed.

We moped around. We hardly communicated with one another, barely talked with words. We had nothing to talk about, really. There was no need to say anything. We were both grieving. My father was in bad shape. I didn't realize it then. I was so gone myself, so self-absorbed, so concerned with my own survival, that I couldn't reach out to anyone else, not even him—especially him. He was devastated, still is more than twenty years on, by the death of his wife. He didn't know what to do with himself. He was lost, grappled with his own personal demons. He didn't have the verbal means or intellectual capacity to exteriorize that lostness, to talk about it, to express it, to release it. Neither did I.

So that night we sat outside the Norfolk Arms pub, on a wooden picnic bench. It was a balmy summer's evening, one of those special London summer's evenings when everyone is out on the street, usually drinking too much, making happy noise. We just cradled our pints forlornly, staring off into space, sat there just sitting. I remember somebody I sort of knew came by. I wanted to know her more. She lived along Sandwich Street, close to the pub, a block over from Marchmont Street. She liked the area and rented a little flat with her boyfriend. She was doing a Ph.D. at the same institution where I taught, on a different theme to what I taught, something I knew nothing about. She spent a lot of time in southern Spain, digging dry ground. She collected soil samples. I was an urbanist, I told her, wore a brown leather jacket and a plaid checked shirt to prove it. Just like Kerouac.

I saw her at the occasional seminar, stumbled upon her sometimes in the corridor. Her name was Corinna, a nice name. I took a shining to her. I liked how she looked—petite, slim, with shoulder-length light-brown hair, thin features, pretty, compact in her dress, sexy—and how she expressed herself: direct and bold. She'd always stick up her hand and ask a question at those seminars, frequently a probing question. She was smart and feisty, opinionated though never arrogant. If anything, I sensed in her an under-confidence. When she passed by that night we had a warm conversation. She was making dinner, she said. She asked how I was doing. Okay, I'd probably said. Though likely she knew I wasn't. As she walked away, down the street, bidding me goodnight, I started to scheme how I could get together with her. I needed to somehow, had to.

But how? Was it carnal, just lust? Or was I thinking about thinking about love? Was she the One. I wasn't sure. Yet I felt something stir that sad, gloomy summer's night in London. Something happened at the intersection of life. Was it one of those chance urban encounters so precious to the Surrealists, like André Breton meeting Nadja? A contingency becoming an urgency? "I had just crossed an intersection whose name I don't know," Breton wrote in *Nadja* (1928). "Suddenly, perhaps ten feet away, I saw a young woman. She had noticed me, too. She carried her head high, unlike everyone else on the sidewalk. And she looked so delicate she scarcely seemed to touch the ground as she walked. A faint smile may have been wandering across her face… Without a moment's hesitation, I spoke to this unknown woman, though I must admit that I expected the worst."

Nadja told Breton she was "a soul in limbo." I understood what she meant. I was in limbo then as well. I'd even had a chance encounter with somebody else, an undergraduate, a young woman I was teaching. She took my class on "Modernism and the City," basically my excuse to read Marshall's *All That Is Solid Melts into Air*, and get others to read it. I loved teaching Marshall's book; and, as far as I could tell, students loved it, too. I'd go through each chapter with them, get them to read Marshall on Dostoevsky, Goethe, Baudelaire, and Marx. We would read *Notes from Underground*, *The Communist Manifesto*, *Faust*, read about Paris, St. Petersburg, and New York, relating it all to modern London, to my life, to their lives. Then I'd add my own bits and pieces, bring in other readings, Kerouac's *On the Road*, Ginsberg's *Howl*, Rushdie's *The Satanic Verses*, and Jacobs's *Death and Life of Great American Cities*.

More than that, Marshall's book was personally meaningful, written by a man who knew something about loss but who hadn't given up hope, didn't return his entrance ticket to the universe. Instead, he kept on keeping on, and wrote a book affirming life in the maelstrom, where things really did melt into air, often right in front of your nose. Modern people, Marshall said, make their home in this maelstrom, come what may. They struggle to make this one fragile life their own. "There's a vital experience," Marshall said, "an experience of space and time, of the self and others, of life's possibilities and perils, that is shared by men and women all over the world today. I will call this body of experience 'modernity.' To be modern is to find ourselves in an environment that promises us adventure, power, joy, growth, and, at the same time, that threatens to destroy everything we have, everything we know, everything we are."

I never thought the relationship with my student exploitative. She was understanding, mature, helpful, very clever. I needed her company. It was undemanding. I respected her. There was an age gap, for sure. I was the teacher, of course. But we enjoyed each other. I appreciated her. We had fun, hit it off in bed. When we weren't together, I'd think about her. She'd come by every Saturday afternoon, and stay over. I'd cook or we'd go out and eat. I'd always pay. I seemed to have more money than I do now. We both knew it was only a fling, something short-term, temporary, with no strings attached. But I began to find a weird happiness in London then. I began to experience the city in a different light. I'd forgotten I was living in its center. Other people needed to remind me of my good fortune amidst my bad luck. I'm not sure I was ever in love with her. It was more physical, impulsive and compulsive.

I think Corinna found out about my fling, didn't approve. It soon became common knowledge around the department. If ever we bumped into one another, at the copier, at coffee breaks, we chattered. I sensed she might like me. She'd have had to be mad not to sense how I liked her. I prattled on nervously in her company, awkwardly reenacting the balcony scene from *Annie Hall*, when Alvy (Woody Allen) babbles on to Annie (Diane Keaton). "Christ," Alvy's inner voice says, revealed to us as a subtitle, "I sound like FM radio. Relax." "I don't know what I'm saying, she senses I'm shallow." "I wonder what she looks like naked?" Then, musing to herself, Annie: "God, I hope he doesn't turn out to be a schmuck like all the others." So it went, and how it felt for me with Corinna. Christ, I hope she doesn't think *I* am a schmuck like all the others.

We spoke about my work—or lack of it—and I asked about hers, work she thought herself ill-suited to, and about the other night's seminar we'd both attended, about movies I'd seen, movies she'd seen. I went often to the movies, *very* often, almost obsessively, to the Renoir, which was practically next door to my apartment. I remember seeing Wong Kar-wai's *Chungking Express* five nights in a row. I told Corinna about it, how it bowled me over, how ROMANTIC it was. I said it was a great romance with the city, with Hong Kong. And Tony Leung, I almost said, with his hound-dog melancholy, expressed the same unrequited love for Faye as I do for you. They are both dreamers, like the two of us.

Faye serves at a food kiosk near Chungking Mansions along Nathan Road in Kowloon. She dreams of California, has her boom box blast out The Mamas & The Papas' "California Dreamin." She loves playing it loud, the louder the better, she says, because "it stops me thinking." All around her is intense urban life, intensely lived out in public, on the street, where the boundaries between private intimacy and public visibility are porous. They intermingle and people aren't ashamed of it. *Chungking Express* is a paean to urban public life, to its romance, to how people find precious meaning in urban cracks, in micro spaces.

The film also immortalizes Chungking Mansions, a seventeen-story block of cheap apartments and guest rooms, many windowless. Not really any mansion we could imagine, more a rabbit warren for poor temporary workers from South Asia, Sub-Saharan Africa, the Middle East, and the Caribbean; for asylum seekers running for their lives; for hardy backpackers searching gritty, inexpensive adventure. As many as four thousand people stay at Chungking Mansions at one time, over a hundred nationalities. At ground level, budget eateries serve every ethnic food under the sun; outlets deal in recycled cell phones; wholesale clothing stores peddle counterfeit designer labels; drug dealers and prostitutes lurk somewhere in between. Chungking Mansions is a central node for quasi-legal trading and trafficking across the developing world, linking Bangkok to Dubai, Kathmandu to Kampala, Lagos to Dacca, Guangzhou to Mombasa, Karachi to Accra. All of it flows through Chungking Mansions, low-end globalization at the intersection of the world.

When I saw Corinna again she told me she'd seen *Chungking Express* and really liked it. I took this as a minor success, one romantic appreciating another. Then, one night, a few weeks on again, after a departmental seminar, we all piled into a deadbeat central London pub, and later ended up in Wagamama's in Bloomsbury. There was a group of us and because we lived close to one another we finished the night by walking home together. I'd doubtless had too much to drink so I started to pour my heart out, heavily, about my mother's death, and, moreover, about how I felt for her, Corinna. She told me she was with somebody. She was flattered by my pass, kind of felt something for me, too, she said. But circumstances being what they were, she wasn't sure. She didn't think it would be possible for us to see each other. She was sure. She was with someone. The fact she'd repeated her insistence made me think she mightn't be so sure after all. It's true, she said, he mightn't be the right guy, likely he wasn't. She might do better, she said. But she'd made an investment in the relationship.

I remember that word "investment." It struck me as a curious term, a strange surrogate for love. He was a young business guy, did something ridiculous with gas, some scam or another with his partner, another young guy, profiting from Thatcherite deregulation of the utilities industry. It didn't sound right. *He* didn't sound right, I think I said. She was a budding intellectual, waiting in the wings, who'd not had the right encouragement nor been around the right people to release her potential, to let it develop, to do the interesting things I knew she wanted to do. Of course, I was the person she needed, the one who could help! Why opt for crassness, a guy interested only in money?

I wasn't convinced her relationship would last. I *had* to believe it wouldn't last, that I could wean her off this guy, that she would come over to me. I had a mission now, pledged it to myself.

Our paths crossed again soon after, quite by chance, outside Russell Square tube station. I'd just seen off my undergraduate friend, late Sunday afternoon, literally kissed her goodbye when, all of a sudden, I happened upon Corinna exiting the station. She'd wondered what I was doing there loitering around. I think she'd suspected I'd been with *her*. I remember wishing I'd been with Corinna. Things needed to stop between me and the undergraduate. They were coming to a stop, cooling off. I sensed she was cooling off with me, that there was some organic ending looming. She'd had enough with me, I thought, and wanted out.

I kept pushing Corinna for a date, asking her to come for a drink sometime, asking her casually, as if it weren't really a serious date, you know, just a drink between friends. Something like that. Maybe a coffee. She didn't drink coffee, she said. Bad sign. Then, one day, she agreed. It was hard to believe. We met up at the Dôme café along Long Acre. It was crowded but we found a seat and spoke about London. She'd found London disappointing. Most people around her despised London, she said, didn't want to be here, yearned for something more conventional, a big house in a little town. They'd come here for jobs and would go anyplace else for those jobs. She'd come to London for intellectual stimulation, for existential adventure, for the unknown, to meet interesting types, to have intense conversations about books and ideas. But it never happened.

She hadn't found the right company, I said. It's probably why she stuck with that guy, I thought, because she believed she couldn't find anyone or anything better, settled for safety in the light that it could be worse. She told me she was reading Albert Camus's *The First Man*, just published in English. It is Camus's unfinished novel, his most autobiographical. The manuscript had been discovered in 1960, in the wreckage of the fancy sports car that had smashed into a tree on a drizzly afternoon on January 4. Camus died instantly in that car, aged forty-six; the driver, Camus's rich publisher friend, Michel Gallimard, died five days later, never regaining consciousness. The manuscript lay buried for decades, withdrawn by Camus's family; few knew anything about it until Camus's daughter, Catherine, who was fourteen at the time of her father's death, decided the world should see it, despite its incomplete state.

Corinna loved Camus, loved his dusty evocations of windswept Algeria. It reminded her of southern Spain, she said, where she loved to go and dig alone, dreaming under a blazing sun, feeling that fireball warm her bare body, exorcising the dull London chill. Now she started to talk as she'd wanted to talk, like she didn't very often talk: candidly, not afraid or ashamed to talk seriously, to talk passionately. Often she said it either scared people or they'd belittle her, laugh it off with a joke, as if intensity frightened them, unnerved them. I said it probably did. I told them that a writer I admired, John Berger, had to leave Britain because people thought him "indecently intense." Intensity wasn't the English way.

The First Man is Camus's *In Search of Lost Time*, the recreation of his Algerian childhood, his love for his illiterate mother, the schoolteacher who saved him from ignorance, the rebellious freedom he found in Algiers, the smells and sounds of North Africa, Arab pastries, soccer matches, the sea, the desperate poverty and decaying despair. Camus's alter ego, Jacques Cormery, utters one glorious line that sums up my own feeling about life, about its meaning and lack of meaning. I'm sure Raymond Carver wouldn't have disagreed. "You're right," says Cormery, talking over dinner with his old pal Victor Malan. "I've loved life, I'm hungry for it. At the same time, life seems horrible to me, it seems inaccessible. That's why I am a believer, out of skepticism. Yes,

I want to believe, I want to live, forever." Thereafter, Camus says, Cormery "fell silent."

Corinna told me she'd hurt her foot running, had a sore instep, a strain of some kind. In former days, I told her I was a runner myself, a good one, especially adept at running away. So I knew a bit about injuries. Show me, I said. She slipped off her shoe and I felt her foot, began to massage it a little, getting aroused. She let me. It was the first time I'd ever touched her, not exactly flesh but stocking. How's that? I asked. I'd located the source of pain, the point of inflammation. Here I was no longer reenacting *Annie Hall*. Now it was *Chungking Express*, when Faye strains her foot and Tony Leung gives her a massage. Likewise a beautiful, sexy, understated scene. At that moment, with Camus, with the foot massage, with our intellectual outpourings, oblivious to everybody, in a noisy Dôme café, I think we both knew: *this was it*.

London opened out to both of us thereafter. She split with her guy, asked him to move out. I didn't exactly move in but spent evenings at hers. She cooked wonderful dinners, spoke about her passion for food, how she'd been the cook of her household, aged eighteen, after her mother died, aged forty-nine, of colon cancer. Her mother was a big foodie, discovered French food when she'd au paired in the south of France for a summer. Food had been the mainstay of her short life. She'd passed this love on to her daughter, even while they fought a lot. And then her mother went and died before they'd reconciled. We were both motherless.

Our first real date together was doubly important. I'd bought two tickets to see one of my heroes perform at Royal Festival Hall on the South Bank, someone I'd never seen live before: Spalding Gray. This was the debut of Corinna and me. I was introducing her into my world. She was curious to learn more. I didn't force it on her. I was going to see Spalding Gray, and with Corinna. Two people dear to me, dear in different ways, now conjoining. It was a Friday evening, the day after my thirty-seventh birthday.

I was so excited waiting in line to enter the auditorium. I was there early, eager and jittery. The line was long. People straggled out onto the promenade next to the Thames. I hoped Corinna would arrive soon. The line was edging indoors, and I knew that once we were in, in our seats, and Gray had commenced, cleared his throat for the first time, nobody would be allowed late entry. I began to get tense as 7:30 struck. The show was due off at 7:45. Still no signs of Corinna anywhere. I got worried. I'd have to choose soon. Go in alone, or be loyal, wait for Corinna, and, if she's late, miss the show. I got *really* edgy as 7:40 approached. She wasn't about. Maybe she'd mistaken the venue?

I remember the previous evening telling her all about Spalding Gray. Who was he? she'd wondered. How to describe what he did? I wondered. He was a monologist, I said. What's a monologist? she said. Someone who sits behind a desk with a glass of water, I said, and, without props or fancy effects, for an hour-and-a-half talks about themselves in front of an audience. Oh, she said. He tells stories, I said, that make people laugh and think and sometimes cry. He tells of his everyday adventures, his inner thoughts, his doubts and hang-ups, his euphoric moments. He's hilarious, I said.

But, listen, I said, he's no stand-up (or sit-down) comic: this is profound existential and psychological inquiry, "a way of taking full responsibility for my life," Gray says, "and also a more therapeutic way of splitting off a part of myself to observe another part." People can relate to what he says, I said. They find him funny—darkly, ironically, hypochondriacally funny. Here is ego and id dialoguing with one another, doing it in public. What Gray says is both rehearsed and improvised, structured and destructured, depending on his mood, depending on the audience's reactions. No monologue is ever the same, even if it's the same monologue. It's always a work in progress; the wheels spin each night.

Gray comes from Barrington, Rhode Island, I said; but his angst, his self-dramatizing hyperbole, his arrogances and insecurities, make him, for me, quintessentially a New Yorker. "For thirty-four years I lived with you," he once said of his adopted hometown, "and came to love you. I came to you because I loved theater and found theater everywhere I looked. I fled New England and came to Manhattan, that island off the coast of America, where human nature was king and everyone exuded character and had big attitude. You gave me a sense of humor because you are so absurd."

I can't wait to see him in person, I said, I'll be peeing my pants on the night. It's so cool he's coming to town and we can see him together. I've read all his books, seen his monologues on film, like *Swimming to Cambodia*, imbibed them. I remember Gray saying somewhere that he used to read a lot of Raymond Carver, read Carver all the time and couldn't get Carver's writer's voice out of his head. So Gray said the hell with it, I'll use my own recorded voice, which came out sort of like Carver's anyway, a natural voice, breathing its own rhythms.

Gray made New York home in 1967. He got involved with its underground experimental theater community, under Antonin Artaud's and Jerzy Grotowski's spell; and with Liz LeCompte, Gray's girlfriend at the time, joined Richard Schechner's Performance Group. A few years on, he and LeCompte broke off to form the Wooster Group, headquartered at a grungy loft space, the Performing Garage, along Wooster Street in SoHo. The troupe and the venue quickly became the springboard for Gray's monologue career. What if I spoke my own words, he wondered, instead of somebody else's? What if I used myself to play myself? What if, he joked, "I began playing with myself?"

The Wooster Group became Gray's first audience. He'd perform short monologues in front of its members, twenty-minute stints in which he'd unearth childhood memories and reminiscences of his mother, her decent into madness and eventual suicide at fifty-two. These performances, sat behind a simple wooden table, became the beginnings of public autobiography. Each day, "when I'd come in for rehearsal," Gray said, "they would ask me to tell it [the monologue] again, and I did, while Liz taped it. Each day it was embellished and edited and grew as a text until at last we transcribed it."

The big breakthrough came with *Swimming to Cambodia*, a watershed monologue, still his best-known, a virtuoso performance mixing personal and political history—the story of a genocide, a film about that genocide, and Gray's bit role in that film about that genocide. Gray became the US ambassador in Roland Joffé's 1984 Oscar-winning *The Killing Fields*, about two *New York Times* reporters who'd uncovered the US's secret bombing of Cambodia in the early 1970s. The covert campaign was designed to drive the Vietcong out of Cambodia yet instead only stirred things up. The Vietcong retreated to the Cambodian bush, hitched up with a bunch of ruthless guerrillas—the Khmer Rouge, led by Pol Pot—who then initiated the worst auto-homeo-genocide in modern history, the said Killing Fields.

Gray's monologue was about this movie and this real human tragedy. Soon afterward, his monologue about this movie became a movie about his monologue. In November 1986, director Jonathan Demme shot two consecutive performances of Gray's *Swimming to Cambodia* before a live audience at the Performing Garage, as close as you could get to being there without actually being there. At first Demme wasn't turned on. "Before I'd seen Spalding perform," he confessed, "I was horrified at the idea of being trapped in a room with just one person speaking at a desk. I didn't want to see him, even though everyone kept telling me how much I'd love him. When I finally did go to one of his shows I was instantly won over."

The film's prologue is my favorite scene. There, we track Gray pacing Lower Manhattan's streets, notebook under arm, en route to his performance. He looks like the struggling artist he is, or at least was then: forlorn, a bit down at heel, traipsing across Canal Street amid speeding traffic, piled up garbage and graffiti, greatcoat collar turned up; a Dostoevskian underground man fighting off his existential chills. But there's a slyness about him, too, a sprightliness to his gait, an air of anticipation and optimism, bobbing up and down merrily to Laurie Anderson's jaunty soundtrack. Moments later he approaches the steel entrance door of the Performing Garage, with its green sign overhead almost winking at us. Next thing he's on stage, sitting at trademark desk, sipping water, taking a deep breath, ready to begin.

This was 1980s New York. I knew from Marshall that living for the city in that decade had been rough. Fiscal crisis still bit deep into public budgets; factories were closing; decline and hard drugs expressed themselves out on the street, scarred the city's fabric, even as Wall Street boomed and financiers laughed all the way to the bank. Ironically, crisis meant that abandoned old industrial spaces, like the Performing Garage itself, were affordable for a while, to struggling artists who sometimes made great art amongst the debris, in these ruins, without hot water.

I remember seeing this same 1980s New York cityscape before, elsewhere on film, in *My Dinner with André*, which similarly starts off with a theater guy—Wally Shawn—trudging through Lower Manhattan, similarly in a greatcoat, similarly surrounded by blight, litter, and bleak emptiness, similarly crossing Canal Street. As Wally walks we hear his voice-over dialoguing with himself, telling us of his artistic woes: "The life of a playwright is tough," he says. "It's not easy, as some people seem to think. You work hard writing plays, and nobody puts them on. You take up other lines of work to try and make a living—acting, in my case—and people don't hire you. So you spend your days crossing the city back and forth doing the errands of your trade."

I didn't tell Corinna that evening how my acquaintance with Gray first came about through Marshall, through *All That Is Solid Melts into Air*. She'd never heard of Marshall yet. I'd never heard of Spalding Gray till I'd read Marshall: like so much in the latter's treasure trove of a book, Gray was another stimulating idea. I've followed up on them, still follow up on them, and have tracked down many of Marshall's riffs and references. I've tried to live out my own book within Marshall's book, tried to make his literary allusions my real-life allusions, like Marshall suggested you should. "Bringing it all back home," is how Marshall described it, borrowing from one of his own heroes, Bob Dylan. So I brought it back home, whenever I could.

Marshall said Gray's early play, *Rumstick Road*, developed between 1975-1978 as part of the Wooster Group's *Three Plays in Rhode Island*, was "a powerful confrontation with home and with ghosts." *Rumstick Road*, after Gray's childhood home address, tries to understand his mother, her malaise and gradual disintegration, his family as well as Gray himself, as a child and as an adult, as a man-child—"to live with what he knows and with what he will never know," Marshall said. Its dialogue speaks to anybody who'd lost somebody, especially one's mother. In *Rumstick Road*, Gray for the first time talks directly to the audience, dramatizes his dreams and reveries; there's dance, abstract movement, and music; original reel and audio recordings of his mother and father and grandmother, even of his mother's shrink (with Gray miming his words); and photos and slides of his family and two brothers, all seemingly hunky-dory in suburban Rhode Island, circa the 1950s.

Rumstick Road, said Marshall, suggests that "a kind of liberation and reconciliation is possible for human beings in this world." This liberation can never be total, Marshall thought, "but it is real, and earned: Gray has not merely looked into the abyss but gone into it and brought its depths up into the light for us all. Gray's fellow actors have helped him: their intimacy and mutuality, developed through years of work as a close ensemble, are absolutely vital in his labor of discovering and facing and being himself." Still, the play, and the actual experience of his mother's suicide, would remain an open wound for Spalding Gray. How could it be otherwise? For much of his youth, he remembers trying to help his mother through long periods of depression. She might suddenly turn to him and ask: "How shall I do it, dear? How shall I do it? Shall I do it in the garage with the car?"

An emerald apparition approached, flapping in the breeze. An immaculate conception legging toward me, like a blast of verdant light. A sight I shall never forget, arriving just in the nick of time, with barely a minute to spare. She was wearing her new green jacket, bought that very afternoon, especially for the occasion, a special occasion almost missed. But she'd made it, apologized for her tardiness. So much to do today, she said, and she took time out to go clothes shopping, too. Had to run all the way across Waterloo Bridge. She was here, Corinna, and now we could *both* go in, take our seats, ready ourselves for the monologue Spalding Gray was calling *It's a Slippery Slope*.

It was a packed house, over a thousand people. I never knew he had so many UK fans. The atmosphere was electric. I had to admit, and did admit it to Corinna, that I was terribly nervous; not about being with Corinna so much, but nervous that she might be disappointed with Spalding Gray, that she wouldn't like him. And I was nervous he'd fluff his lines, that something would go wrong, and *I* would be disappointed. There was a sudden hush, and then he appeared, discretely, very unspectacularly. Yet there he was, sure enough, Spalding Gray, in the flesh, wearing a red and gray checked flannel shirt. He sat down and paused, calmly took a sip of water, looked up, and then, in a dulcet voice very familiar to me, said: "The first mountain I ever remember seeing was framed in the pane of my geometry class window at Fryeburg Academy in Maine in 1956."

After a couple of moments I knew he was going to be just fine. Skiing no longer became a gray area: now it was a Gray area, a tale of a midlife crisis, of a man trying to find his balance in life and on skis, a man who, no matter what, "was always a little bit not present." "I'm tired of being a VICARIAN," Gray told his partner Renée. "I want to live a life, not tell it! I want to turn right on skis!" At a ski lesson, he's the only one in class who can't turn right. Right, left, right, left, they all went, snaking gently down the bunny slope. While he: left, left, left, then right, left, right…then *bam*, down he went, into the snow. Just a simple shift of weight was all you needed, and you could turn right, then left, then right again, and left—"Oh my God, Spalding," his inner cheerleader voice began saying, at those rare moments of equilibrium, "you're skiing!" Then: CRASH! He'd be in the snow again. "If I was not whole and completely there and balanced on my skis," Gray said, "I would be DOWN! The mountain would HIT me hard." A metaphor about existence, maybe, for a life full of sharp twists and turns, hard bumps and tight corners. You need to be able to wiggle every which way to keep your balance.

There was a lot going on in Gray's life just then. Before long, the monologue took on a serious, almost painful tone. Off *piste*, things were more unbalanced. He spoke about his own suicidal tendencies, fantasies about how he was going to do it, now that he was fifty-two himself, the age his mother ended it all. "I was reversing my history," he said. "Mom was no longer going mad, my inner kid was going mad and saying, 'Hey, Mom! Hey, Renée, look at this—look at what it looks like to go crazy.' The craziness manifested itself in imitations of Mom's behavior, or my actually becoming like her." He said he was beginning to act up in public places, much the same way his mom acted up. "I'd be muttering to myself," he said, "and involuntarily shouting out." Yet this was New York City, and nobody really noticed or cared. Or if they did notice, they joined in. "I can remember screaming in the streets at night," Gray said, "and hearing my scream picked up by other people who passed it on down the street for blocks and blocks. What started out as real panic was turned into a performance by the people."

When I heard this, I thought it a tremendously affecting eulogy to New York. The city could participate in a collective reenactment of Aristotle's *Poetics*: acting out tragic drama, people engaged in a public *catharsis*, like Aristotle suggested theater should be—a communal release, a cry for HELP, a cleansing of tragedy. "When Mom let out a few of these yelps in a Rhode Island supermarket," Gray said, "they put her in a straitjacket and gave her shock treatments. *If Mom had lived in New York City, she'd still be alive today*." This was the killer line. Maybe it's the most important item we should talk about when we talk about cities. Cities should release repression rather than enforce it. There, in the streets, we bring our worst feelings to the surface and work through them as a public. Maybe I should have gotten out of my café a while ago, gone onto Marchmont Street, and yelled my head off. Could London have taken it like New York?

Gray's personal life was getting complicated and self-destructive. He confessed to an affair he'd had, was still having, with a younger woman called Kathie; and she was pregnant with his child. But he doesn't want the kid, doesn't want to be a father, tells Kathie "get rid of it." He acts crummily, is in denial. On a whim he marries longtime girlfriend Renée, consummating a relationship they'd begun in 1979, hoping it would extinguish the burning hot affair, and refreshen a stale relationship—Renée, like Liz LeCompte before her, wasn't only Gray's confidante and lover; she was also his theatrical soulmate and creative advisor, almost his business manager. Yet the affair heats up even more. Renée has had enough, hears about the pregnancy, leaves Gray, clears out of their SoHo loft. Gray goes to see Kathie and his eight-month-old son, Forrest, and suddenly has the exhilarating experience of fatherhood; a new life as a family man beckons. "Bending over him,

I looked down into his eyes, and fell in. I did not expect the gaze that came back, it was absolutely forever. Long, pure, empty, mere being, pure consciousness, the observing self that I'd always been trying to catch was staring back at me; they were no-agenda eyes."

Kathie moves into his loft with her seven-year-old daughter, Marissa. Now, with Forrest, they are a foursome; domestic chaos is thrust upon him. But it's maybe a first glimpse of real happiness, even of contentment, of being there and only there. And *there* it seems like he's come to life again, earned the sort of liberation that Marshall had hinted at; never total, but real. Out skiing in Vermont, at the end of the day, at the end of his monologue, alone in contemplation, he skis through the twilight like a demon. Left, right, left, right he goes, tucking behind a seventy-year-old man, who is "skiing the most beautiful, carved, Tai Chi-like turns." "And later I bid him farewell," Gray said, "knowing I have seen both a person and an apparition, the spirit of the future."

Gray thought he was undergoing a meltdown, was self-destructing, disintegrating. But instead he brought new life into the world, rejuvenated, grew up, accepted responsibility for his new creation, and for being a grown-up. There was a split and then a fusion, a passionate embrace. For that he gave himself a big high-five. "I knew now," he said, "that I had to stay alive to help this little guy through."

Exiting the auditorium I was dying to know what Corinna thought. She could see I was ebullient, thrilled by the experience, absolutely *not* disappointed. But what about her? I'd heard her laugh a few times, giggle at Spalding a bit. Then she turned to me and said she'd really enjoyed it, didn't understand everything, but that he was great. She said he was special. He was *brave*, she said. You mean confessing in public? I said. No, not really that, she said. It's just the idea of sitting there alone, at a desk, talking to lots of people without anything. That was brave. There's nothing to protect you from flopping. It's so low-tech, isn't it, I said, in a world saturated by technology. Nobody would ever believe it possible. Engaging an audience like that.

We're so used to seeing flashing images, shifting images, loud, pulsating music and dramatic effects and gimmicks. We've almost lost the ability to sit still and listen to somebody tell a story, one human being communicating with other human beings, without mediation, through language and nothing else. It was how Wordsworth said a poet should address their audience: "using the language of real men," "a man speaking to man." It was why Gray didn't really like his monologues becoming films. It was real life he was after, not reel life. Although, you know, he's a bit weird, isn't he, Corinna said, a bit strange. I guess it was true. Most people I love are strange, a bit weird somehow.

Years later, she told me what she liked most about things then, about seeing Spalding Gray and others, was how it was all new and unknown to her, a great adventure; being exposed to it was a thrill and a pleasure. That was what was most important, even if she didn't get it all, or even if she didn't like everything. I mean, she said, he was a shit toward his old girlfriend, Renée, wasn't he, how he'd betrayed her, cheated on her, abandoned any sense of loyalty. It was all immediate gratification for him. Selfish, just about him, she'd said, any woman could see that. His monologues were definitely stories for guys. He's a bit too obsessed with sex, she'd said.

We did see Spalding Gray perform again a couple of years on, at Lincoln Center, after we'd moved to New York, a new monologue, *Morning, Noon and Night*, about a single day in the life of his new domesticity, Gray's Joycean moment. Now, he became a sort of Leopold Bloom, an ironical Everyman. He'd had another kid, another boy, Theo, only a few months old, moved to the east end of Long Island, to the quaint town of Sag Harbor, buying an old house next to a whalers' church, straight out of the opening scenes of *Moby-Dick*. It was a strange odyssey he'd recounted that night at the Vivian Beaumont Theater, a charming, less conflicted and angst-ridden tale about the daily round of fatherhood, bike riding with Forrest, eating ice cream together, meals and bath time with Theo, an ordinary life made a little less ordinary through the wave of Gray's magic wand.

But then something terrible happened. In June 2001, he was in Ireland celebrating his sixtieth birthday, out driving one night with friends, along a deserted country road, with Kathie at the wheel and Spalding in the back. Out of nowhere, at a sleepy junction, a speeding mini-van, driven by a local vet, struck them head-on. Gray, who wasn't wearing a seatbelt, broke his hip and smashed his forehead against the back of Kathie's head; both were unconscious for a while. Kathie seemed okay, suffering only bruises and minor injuries, nothing permanent. But Gray couldn't walk; his head swelled up. He had hip surgery, sciatic nerve damage, which left him with a numb foot.

Bone fragments pressed against the right frontal lobe of his brain, the part that enables you to think reflectively and maintain steady focus. It seemed he had brain damage. Titanium plates were fitted. His face was disfigured and he could no longer walk properly, no longer hike nor ski. Nor, apparently, could he do his monologues as before. Gray sunk into a deep depression, deeper than ever. Meanwhile, he decided to sell his old Sag Harbor house, the one lovingly depicted in *Morning, Noon and Night*, buying another newer and bigger property nearby, more practical for his enlarged family. Immediately, though, regret seized him. Selling it had been "catastrophic." He tried to buy it back. But the new owners weren't interested. His depression worsened. Then he started to leave suicide notes on the kitchen table.

Gray had been a depressive most of his adult life, like me. In early 2004, when I was living in France, I learned he'd finally gone through with it, had committed suicide. It was a bitter blow, crushing for my own wobbly midlife. With his watery disappearance in New York Harbor, after throwing himself off the Staten Island Ferry, in bleak mid-winter late one night, part of my New York drowned, too. Poor Spuddy Gray. He could tell a life but couldn't quite live a life. How he tried. I hope it doesn't happen to me.

In Ray Carver's stories, he's able to move fast through time because he compresses peoples' life history into the space of several short paragraphs. Afterward, his art homes in on the detail he thinks important: a conversation over a cup of coffee, a silence between lovers, a bitter fight between a couple whose marriage seems to have failed even before they've honeymooned. All else is structure, mere background; he's into particularity. In two or three sentences, you're already married with teenage kids, and about to part company. Suddenly, a line on, it's a Sunday evening and you're sitting on the couch, and the radio is on in the kitchen. Then the real action begins.

I'm not sure I can work that fast or with that level of detail. It's true that me and Corinna were in love. That was the crux of things, what we wanted to talk about. But it was something we also wanted to build a practical life around. We both began to see the city through different eyes, through shared eyes. We expressed a joint compact, a dream of a life together, an adventurous life together. Come live with me and be my love. There was no point in Corinna paying rent, I said, so why not move in with me. She did for a while. Then we thought we'd buy a bigger place, a little farther east, close to Exmouth Market in Clerkenwell. It was still a bit run down over there, but very much up and coming. A restaurant called Moro had just opened, along with a few new coffee shops that jarred with the old greasy spoons.

The place we found had two floors, a basement and a ground floor, an ex-council maisonette, part of an old Georgian terrace. We repainted and redid it all together. I suppose we were gentrifiers of sorts, putting in sweat equity, exhausting work. We were emboldened by our dream, by our life as a couple, investing in a romance not real estate. We had black and white checkered lino laid down in the kitchen, bought a retro diner set of table and chairs, painted the walls green all round, mounting a large framed-print of Edward Hopper's *Automat*, which gave off a green hue, just the right green we were looking for. We were trying to create our own automat, there in our own kitchen.

That Hopper painting was first unveiled on Valentine's Day, 1927. It was part of an exhibition staged at New York's Rehn Gallery. We both loved the image; its romance was never lost on us. (Nor the date of its unveiling. Apparently, Hopper modeled it after his wife, Jo.) A lone, well-dressed woman sat late at night in a cafeteria, in an automat. She looks isolated and vulnerable, rejected by her lover, or maybe yet to find the right lover. We both agreed the woman was beautiful; she reminded me of Corinna, who sometimes looked sad like that. Her sadness would always come from her mother's premature death. Corinna wore a floppy hat like the woman's, too. And, of course, she wore a green jacket like hers, one I'll always remember coming toward me, the night of the Spalding Gray show; the same green jacket that flapped in the breeze.

We painted the living room bright turquoise and gold. I wanted it to be over the top, striking, and Deco like something out of *The Great Gatsby*, something wild and crazy out of Scott Fitzgerald. We were Scott and Zelda, after all, putting on the Ritz, so why not. Down below, we had a bedroom that got its theme from a Modigliani nude we had, a giant print of a reclining woman depicted in luscious crimson. So we painted the walls a similar deep crimson, fitting for what we hoped would be our dark secret love den, faraway and safe from the hassles of life above us, outside the front door.

We loved what we'd done, yet soon began to hate the apartment for the dread zone it became. Up above we had neighbors from hell. They must have been out each time we'd visited before buying it. There was no sound isolation separating us. Around four every morning, we heard the guy stomping down the stairwell, which ran down the side of our apartment, haring down, slamming the door behind him. Everything reverberated, vibrated like a major-scale earthquake, striking central London. Could he please try to tread a little more gently? we politely enquired. No, he couldn't. Next day, and thereafter, the stomping and slamming were louder than ever.

In the kitchen, morning, noon, and night, we could hear their washing machine penetrate our flimsy ceiling, vividly sounding out each particular cycle of the wash. It never seemed to stop. They had one kid, how much washing could that generate? It was bizarre. Their TV blared out, they crashed about at all hours. They shrieked at us when we asked them to keep it down, to consider us below, as we had once considered them. Before long, I said fuck'm and started to crank up the volume of my music, letting "Misty Mountain Hop" boom out, recruiting John Bonham to drum our revenge. We knew then it was a lost cause, that dream of a home of ours. It felt sullied, desanctified. We knew we had to leave, get out of there.

But we tried to lead a literary life nonetheless. We went to book readings together. I remember we went to see one of Carver's old chums, Richard Ford, give a reading. I knew he was a Carver chum because Ray had written an essay, appropriately labeled "Friendship," about Richard and another mutual writer-friend of theirs, Tobias Wolff. A photo accompanied Carver's text: three men standing and smiling at the camera, Wolff and Ford leaning on the gentle, bear-like giant Carver, happily in the middle, smart in suit and tie, on the wagon but doing just fine tonight. It was taken in London, circa mid-1980s. "There was an elegance about his bearing," Carver said of Ford, "about his clothes, even his speech—which was poised and courtly and southern. I looked up to him, I think, since he was so clearly everything I was not!"

That was how we found Ford that night, too. I expected a pal of Carver's to be a bit more plainmanish, a bit rougher round the edges, more vernacular, raspier. Instead, he wore a snazzy suit and was very stately, with long coiffed hair, combed scrupulously behind his ears. It didn't seem quite right for what he was reading, *Independence Day*, his sequel to *The Sportswriter* he'd published a decade prior, continuing the mishap adventures of Frank Bascombe, a sportswriter-cum-real estate agent. Frank's an ordinary kind of guy, leading an ordinary "applauseless" life, a divorcee, a reluctant middle-ager, with a troubled teenage son,

Ralph, whom Frank goes to visit. They end up, over a long Fourth of July weekend—Independence Day—at the Baseball Hall of Fame at Cooperstown, New York, consecrating an unspoken father and son reconciliation.

Ford read out his text in a slow, southern drawl. It wasn't quite how I imagined Frank sounding. The dialogue and delivery didn't convince me. I bought his book anyway, began reading it, yet soon felt the same way. Too slow going, and, at four hundred and fifty pages, too much of it. I never believed this was an authentic voice coming from the heart, lived out through actual experience, like Carver's. It was more a writer's construction, contrived and conceived, a writer consciously writing a book. His pal Carver gave us more than this, gave us more by saying less, and that extra was what I wanted from my own life and from literature.

A week or so later we saw John Berger at Waterstones in Hampstead. This was almost as big a thrill for me as seeing Spalding Gray. Alas, John *did* fluff it that night. He started off well enough, on good form, dressed in chunky denim work shirt, sleeves rolled up, ready for action, cropped white hair, stocky and earthy looking, cheerily bantering with the audience beforehand, many of whom he seemed to know, or seemed to know him. He certainly looked the part, like someone who lived next door to peasants and who toiled the land once in a while. He was back in the UK for a flash visit, he said, Eurostarring in that very morning, here to promote a special BBC Radio 3 version of his novel, *To the Wedding*.

Some of that novel resembled Spalding Gray's *It's a Slippery Slope*: "Everything's a question of how you lean," explains Berger's motorcyclist alter-ego Jean Ferrero, to daughter Ninon. It's Ninon who recounts papa's lesson as he journeys to her wedding, cross-frontier, *en moto*, to a little village in Italy on the Po Delta; Ninon, the daughter who's just been diagnosed as HIV positive. Berger, the free spirit art critic, novelist, poet, filmmaker, and self-avowed "jack-of-all-trades," denizen of a small Alpine village for the past forty years, likewise rides a giant motorbike, a 1100 cc Honda Blackbird; he knows firsthand that little parable for life: it's all a matter of how you lean into a bend, how you deal with inertia, how you deal with the laws of life's gravity as well as life's grace.

Berger read brilliantly from *To the Wedding*, and went on to speak about the dilemmas of how a novel could be brought to radio, how written words could become spoken words as well as sounds—like the revving up of a motorbike; how the atmosphere of continental Europe, of Alpine passes and deserted villages could come alive without either text or image. How could one particular artistic medium, say, a novel, be readapted for another medium? Berger thought everything possible. The translation or transition doesn't have to be literal; indeed, it shouldn't be literal, he said. There's plasticity and malleability to any great work of art, which allows for creative reworking and imaginative reinvention. Sometimes, he said, something entirely new can be created. One difficulty he faced in readapting this novel for the radio was that its narrator is a blind old Greek man, who sells *tamas* in the street, little metal prayer plaques. This plainly wasn't going to work in radio drama. And so, after much clutching and crunching of his cranium, Berger decided, in a great leap of the imagination, that the narrator should be the River Po itself, Italy's longest waterway, whose gush flows hauntingly through the BBC's broadcast.

At question time, John's good cheer turned sour. In a throwaway comment, he said how he hated Anthony Minghella's recent film adaptation of Michael Ondaatje's *The English Patient*. Ondaatje was a close friend, Berger said, and the film veered unforgivably from the original novel. Its richness, Berger said, was lost. At that point, a member of the audience interjected, and politely wondered whether Berger wasn't contradicting all he'd said hitherto? Wasn't he being hypercritical? What about his comments about artistic license creatively readapting a great work? Surely Ondaatje's *English Patient* could take it, was complex and expansive enough to allow for multiple reinterpretations? To believe only one, sole, *essential* reading of a book, the man queried, didn't that fly in the face of your fundamental point?

True, Minghella decides to focus on a love affair between "English patient" Count László de Almásy (Ralph Fiennes) and nurse Katharine Clifton (Kristin Scott Thomas), as opposed to that between the Sikh sapper Kip (Naveen Andrews) and nurse Hana (Juliette Binoche)—as in Ondaatje's book. But what emerges, it seemed to me at least, is something intimate and wonderfully romantic, a worthy companion to Ondaatje's splendid written word; the final scene with Katherine, in the Sahara's Cave of Swimmers, dying in the arms of Ralph Fiennes, just breaks your heart. When Corinna and I had seen *The English Patient*, not long before, we both collapsed into a flood of tears, devastated, pure emotional meltdown. The thought that this fate might strike Corinna, that one day she might also die in my arms, like Kristin Scott Thomas in the arms of the English patient, was the most heartrending thing I could ever imagine in the whole world. The film so touched us, so overwhelmed us, had me think such thoughts, feel such feelings; how could Berger be so off in his judgment?

Yet instead of accepting the guy's criticism, laughing it off in agreement, Berger got prickly and defensive, aggressively argumentative. Every rejoinder seemed only to dig his own grave more. I think he knew it, but still wouldn't back off. He sounded pompous and snobby, insisting that there was a singular aura around art, especially around his friend's art, and that the film was no good because it was popular. I remember telling Corinna how disappointed I was with him. She thought him "arrogant." For years, I never read anything more he wrote.

It's weird thinking about this now, because I did get back to reading him again, and even, miraculously, got to know him personally. John would call me up sometimes and we'd have long chats on the phone. He said curious things I didn't expect. "Bless you," he'd often say. This was the period when I wrote a book about him. He was tremendously supportive throughout, tremendously encouraging, fifteen years after I'd seen him in Waterstones that disappointing night. After the book's release, he sent me a lovely postcard, with a handwritten note, inscribed in the jet-black ink of his trusty fountain pen, reciting the concluding lines of my book, adding: "*You, the pilot, I, the pillion, cornering not badly at all. Thank you—your bike! John.*"

John and Marshall were the two intellectuals I admired most in the world. Marxist humanists the pair, but Marxist humanists from different tacks. John's "authenticity" came from the countryside, in rural life, from wearing Van Gogh's boots and wallowing in pig earth. His Marxism was full of Proudhonist love of the artisan, mindful of a peasant mode of production that lived on inside modern capitalism. Marshall's authenticity emerged through the city, embraced modern urban life, dealt with it headlong, warts and all. His was a Marxism of the street and the sidewalk, of bright neon lights and big city dreams, of feeling more alive amid masses of people. Confrontation with the city. Marshall said, the exposure of the self to its promises and perils, is the ultimate test of who a person is, of all they might be.

I've often mused whether both uttered a similar refrain, voiced a similar "structure of feeling," a Marxism of feeling, a Marxism of vital experience, of subjectivity. Their humanism put social theory back inside people, inside individuals. So maybe, inside themselves, they had more of each other's humanist sensibility than they would have realized, never knowing one another, living continents apart. Marshall's life was rooted in his great big village of the Upper West Side; and John, no matter how much hay he scythed, could never be anything but a rootless urbane intellectual. Throughout their lives, they secretly enlisted their Other.

The first time Corinna met Marshall was in French Roast, northeast corner of Broadway and West 85th Street. The faux French bistro had been Marshall's choice. It was a sweaty spring morning, drizzly, with a heavy, lingering humidity. I remember this because it was the first thing that struck me when Marshall entered: his rain jacket, an all-weather sports protector, in fluorescent pink! Marshall's style was anti-style, a style all his own. I'd soon learn how he loved bright colors, Day-Glo designs, tie-dye T-shirts, Hawaiian shirts, pinks and greens and turquoises and aquamarines. He wore them as badges of honor, as rainbows arcing his sky; and that day he lit up the bistro in every sense.

It was the first time Corinna had been to New York. It was an important trip for us as a couple, the farthest we'd so far been together. When Marshall heard this he took it upon himself to be the city's cultural ambassador, offering us recommendations about what we should see, current exhibits worth checking out, where to get ace ice cream, fab pasta, a terrific steak, great brunch. New York was *his* responsibility; that's how he felt toward the city. I'd never met anybody who bore a city on his back like he did. It was true love.

Corinna said I was like a kid in a candy store around Marshall. She was enthusiastic and excited about meeting somebody she didn't know because she loved me and saw how enthusiastic and excited I was about meeting him again. It was a big deal for her because it was a big deal for me. She had no real idea who Marshall was, hadn't heard of him before, hadn't read anything he wrote.

I told her he was a luminary figure in urban studies and Marxism, yet a chip off the old block, not your standard academic type. She could tell as soon as she saw him hobble into French Roast, giving us big hugs all round, full of welcoming warmth. He sat down awkwardly, readjusting himself so his bulk could fit the chair.

I'd warned her beforehand he was distinctive looking, like no one else, an Old Testament prophet, short and fat, with a thick curly gray mane and shaggy, flyaway fly. Even though he was wide awake, Marshall frequently looked somnolent, preoccupied, with sad droopy eyes, underscored by huge bags that seemed only to make those eyes droop even more, making him look even sadder. And there were also the holes in his head, from the brain surgery he'd had the previous decade. Sometimes Marshall would tilt his head back and it would sway from side to side as if he couldn't control himself; he'd wriggle around looking like he wasn't fully present, like he was distracted somehow. But he was fully present. He could be slow in talking and responding, and sometimes you had to be patient. He'd ruminate and pause, and you weren't sure if he was going to continue or, if you'd said something, whether he was going to reply. I remember how he once described his old professor, the great liberal critic Lionel Trilling, who taught Marshall as an undergraduate at Columbia University in the late 1950s; Marshall could have been talking about himself: "Lionel was uneasy, brooding, melancholy, full of Beckettesque hesitation about communication."

If Marshall's speech was hesitant, his emotional depth seemed Dostoevskian. He was the Underground Man and Alyosha Karamazov rolled into one, able to commune with higher spiritual powers few of us had any real idea about. Corinna could see how much I looked up to him. I was a journeyman back then, barely published, an ambivalent academic serving my time, needing a role model to help me through that ambivalence. Marshall was the Dude, the Big Lebowski, and wrote and thought the way I wanted to. I knew his work better than anybody's, tracked down everything he did, prowled the university stacks for back copies of the *Nation* or *Dissent*, which in those days were *real*, on actual paper, held in cardboard boxes. I'd spend hours and a small fortune xeroxing them all, annotating them later, putting them away in manila folders, my very own offline hard drive. In discovering Marshall, I was discovering myself.

I think he saw this ambivalence coming partly from my class background, that, like him, I hailed from the working classes, from the urban ruins, also like him. My father similarly left school at twelve without an education. I came of age in the rust belt, in a deindustrialized city that had seen hard times. I'd felt those hard times in my bones. I think he could see I wasn't one of those slouching *Brideshead Revisited* types, living on trust funds and still clinging onto memories of the Empire. As a Liverpool lad I had more in common with him, a Bronx primitive, than with any upper-crust or middle-class Brit. Indeed, I wanted to get out of England because of all that stuff. It seemed to help bond us, despite a twenty-year age gap, despite my not being Jewish. I was a-religious; I'd seen sectarianism fuck things up when I was growing up in Liverpool.

I could see how Marshall always grappled with religion, with the God question. I found this intriguing, something I could strangely identify with. I don't know if it's because I've always felt like a victim, hard done by. I've carried this sensibility around with me, ever since age sixteen. It's meant I've sometimes self-dramatized, been paranoid, neurotic, frequently depressive. I always thought Marshall was the same. He battled it by affirming life, by looking the negative in the face and living with it. I loved that Jewish gallows humor, that chutzpah, that Groucho Marxism: I, too, never wanted to join any club that would have me as a member. Marshall said he started rereading the Bible in the mid-1970s. "I never believed in any god," he said. "But I came to believe that if I was going to grow up, I had to find ways to connect the parts of my life: myself as an adult, with education and a PhD, with myself as a child, in a nonexistent part of the

Bronx. The stories that haunted me then and that still haunt me are about cities. Biblical cities—Jerusalem, of course, but also the pagan cities that surround it, Tyre, Babylon, Damascus—are seen as always vulnerable, their existence tenuous."

"I took it for granted that *I* was vulnerable," he said, "but never imagined that *the city* could be vulnerable, too." He said he came back to live on the Upper West Side in 1967 after a stint away; first at Oxford, then at Cambridge, Massachusetts, at Harvard, doing a doctorate. "My neighborhood was the Upper West Side," Marshall said, "and somehow I hadn't heard about the heroin epidemic that was tearing up Broadway. The gutters were full of syringes; on the sidewalks, the living casualties lurched at you, though more often they crumbled into themselves." As the 1970s ended, "there was a sense of relief in the air, that the city was recovering at last. But the 1980s brought a whole new wave of disasters: masses of homeless people spread out right there on the streets and in the subways, filling up every empty public space; then the AIDS epidemic, and crack cocaine, the first killer drug to crack the mass market, lifting violence to new heights." It was hard to conceive this now, looking at the bright young things at French Roast, and at Victoria's Secret across the street.

Marshall and I both had close encounters with the English ruling classes when we studied at Oxford. I'd done a doctorate there in the late 1980s and early 1990s, won a scholarship to study under the eminent Marxist geographer, David Harvey, whom I got close to. I loved the intellectual stimulation at Oxford, loved being around Harvey and his cohort of smart and fun grad students. But I never got on with the place, never gave myself a chance to get on with the place. It all felt very strange and alien for me, very Other, coming from Liverpool, and *sounding* like I came from Liverpool. I never had that monied poise or arrogance, the sense that I owned the joint, that the world revolved around me. I never would. My arrogance was different. Marshall came to Oxford in 1961, passing a year on a B.Litt., a sort of master's degree, and wrote a thesis supervised by Isaiah Berlin called "Freedom and Individuality in the Thought of Karl Marx." He said he had a great time at Oxford, "a far better time than I could have had at any American graduate school. But I didn't open up to Oxford as a place. I know I loved the architecture, and filled my letters home with sketches of Classic domes, Gothic towers, Romantic parks. But soon it got dark and cold, the gorgeous buildings cast long shadows, and I got lonely and paranoid. I came to feel that the place's very beauty was really there to crush the working class and the Jews and people like me." I'd feel exactly the same way almost three decades on.

That time at Oxford made a lasting impression on Marshall. He'd always be a bit of an Anglophile, steeped in English literature, knew Jane Austen really well, and Dickens and Hazlitt and Charles Lamb, could cite from memory verse by Wordsworth and Donne and Milton. Shakespeare was his dearest love; *King Lear*, "my favorite piece of literature in the whole world." I'd seen an old photo of Marshall when he'd been at Oxford, in his early twenties; and, amazingly, he *does* look the Oxbridge part, *does* look like something out of *Brideshead Revisited*: clean-shaven, short hair, wearing a smart tweed sports jacket and dash tie; dangling nonchalantly, in his left hand—Marshall was left-handed—is what seems like a cigarette but which, as a lifelong non-smoker, is in fact a pen. He'd hold his hand and pen in that exact same manner all his life. It's fascinating to compare this Oxford photo with those of a few years on, after he'd returned to the US. As the Sixties progressed, his body morphed with the times. The tie went, exchanged for open-necked denim, the hair got longer and more unkempt, and the facial hair grew. He'd lightened up, seemingly liberated himself, hippified, was busy being born. Soon, as '68 erupted, he'd have sympathy for the devil.

I remember my first ever contact with Marshall had been at Oxford. I tried to entice him back there for a conference I was co-organizing. It was the only thing I've ever organized in my life, fêting the twentieth anniversary of David Harvey's important book, *Social Justice and the City*. I'd invited Marshall because for a long while I'd admired his work and wanted to meet him; to my amazement he accepted. "I'd love to come!" he'd said in a fax, pre-email. "The title of my paper (presentation)," he'd added, "will be 'Justice/Just Us,' and it will be an attack on some of the forms of tribal particularism that underlie and mangle some current demands for universal justice." Marshall said, "I expect to talk about the world of hip-hop, which I know something about, and maybe I'll play a song or two." Then, at the end of the fax, he said something strange, something revealing, though of what I'm still not sure: "I hope you won't consider me a liberal fuck!"

Marshall did come, donned in bright purple shirt, blue jeans, and beat-up brown leather jacket, a long way from how he'd looked when a student. He did read out his paper on hip-hop and played a few tunes to boot. Although this wasn't quite true: he sang out his own tunes, bawled out refrains from rappers Melle Mel and Chuck D, blending it all together with reading James Joyce's *Ulysses*, where Stephen Dedalus said history is a "shout in the street." Marshall blew everybody's minds that afternoon; not just because of his immense intellect, nor even because of the weird mélange of Machiavellian political theory and black pop culture; more because of his intense honesty and emotional charge, an almost-unbearable frankness in talking about himself.

We didn't get too much chance to talk then. He'd been elusive at the social events, didn't come to the conference dinner at Browns, likely out of shyness and perhaps suspicion. But upon leaving he told me he really enjoyed the occasion, loved coming back to Oxford, and if ever I were in New York, I should look him up. He gave me his number, which I kept. Then I met him that time at Metro Diner. And now here I was at French Roast, with Corinna, and so was he, and Marshall mentioned that at Oxford he'd been tutored by fascinating people, including Iris Murdoch. Corinna said Iris Murdoch had been a family friend. Corinna's late grandmother, Jacquetta Hawkes, was a Murdoch confidant. Jacquetta herself had written novels, and poetry, but had become more well-known for popularizing archeology, in books and on TV and the radio. She was a free-spirited woman *avant la lettre*, also helping kick-start the Campaign for Nuclear Disarmament (CND) with Canon John Collins and his wife Diana. Meantime, Jacquetta was J. B. Priestley's last wife. (Priestley had supported Murdoch's early career.) "Grandpa Jack" was my step-grandfather, Corinna said. Oh, yes, Marshall said, I think I've read two of his ninety books. It seemed Marshall wasn't being entirely complimentary.

Corinna was reticent about this part of her past. Her grandmother was a crushingly intimidating figure. Whenever young Corinna wrote letters, thanking her for the Christmas or birthday present she'd received, Jacquetta would respond correcting

Corinna's spelling and punctuation. John Bayley, Iris's English professor husband, was terrified of Jacquetta, stuttering even more in her company. Jacquetta was super-posh, wealthy in a way Corinna's parents never were. It was all too much for Jacquetta's son, Nicolas, Corinna's father, who was sent off to boarding school, read Classics at Oxford, and later eloped to Africa where he taught Shakespeare in the bush. He was a fervent anti-colonialist and lifelong Quaker, settling for a while in York—Old York!—where Corinna grew up. Corinna's mother and father almost settled in London's Primrose Hill. They'd asked Jacquetta if they could borrow money to buy a house there after they were married. But Jacquetta wouldn't give them any. Snob as she was, in those days she thought Primrose Hill, near to a belching King's Cross, a grubby, soot-ridden part of town, was a "bad investment!" Corinna's grandmother never featured as a source of inspiration: Jacquetta's life was so rarefied, so privileged and brainy—chummy with "Charles" (Chaplin) and "George" (Orwell)—that it bore no resemblance to the reality of Corinna's own upbringing in York. Her poor mother, Corinna lamented, always felt inadequate around Jacquetta.

Corinna later said she enjoyed meeting Marshall, talking to him, listening to him. A lovely, gentle man, she said, a wise man. That's how she described him: *wise*. He was wise, of course. He didn't just know stuff in books like a lot of intellectuals who, despite all their learning, weren't wise in the slightest. With Marshall you sensed he knew stuff about life as well as about books. At first, Corinna said she'd been a bit put off because he was, well, "ugly." Ugly? I queried. Surely it didn't take long to see past this, I said, to go beneath it: there was something beautiful *inside* Marshall, beautiful in the ancient Greek sense, which transcended physical looks, was Socratic, a beauty of the soul.

Marshall was like Socrates, maybe even looked the way Socrates looked: ragged, overweight, a roaming, popular street philosopher from the lower-classes; unlike Plato, who came from the upper-classes. Socrates said the gods appointed him as Athens's special "gadfly." He was there to irritate the city, to bother and bite it, to ensure it kept open all hours, that it was fully awake. Socrates loved Athens, talked to everyone, talked *like* everyone, using non-specialist everyday language. In the *Menexenus*, Plato said Socrates talked to slaves. One time, he stopped a messenger boy and started up a conversation about geometry. The ruffian is interested but says he can't talk to Socrates because he has no education; Socrates says it doesn't matter: the kid is open to ideas like all humans, and that's all that matters. Yet Socrates loved wisdom more than people. Apparently, he never cried, which isn't like Marshall. Marshall knew that in the *agora* you have the right to love as well as talk. And he knew that crying was cool, even for grown-ups.

Corinna said something else about Marshall then that always struck me: he was *opinionated*. He wasn't afraid to speak his mind, she said, to say what he felt not just what he thought, I said. I guess, true to Socrates, he'd have to be opinionated, wouldn't he, because he cared, because he took things to heart as well as to head. Frequently in his work Marshall cited Shakespeare's Edgar, from *King Lear*: "Speak what we feel, not what we ought to say." When he wanted to, Marshall could be scathing with his opinions, sometimes scathingly funny with his opinions, especially when voiced against his peer urbanists. It's almost as if he spoke what he felt when he thought academic urbanists were giving cities a bad name, talking clichés and banalities about urban life. He seemed to take it more to heart when the banalities came from the Left.

Marshall really disliked Richard Sennett, laying into what many believe the latter's magnum opus, *The Fall of Public Man*: "When Sennett isn't looking down on people," Marshall said in *The Nation*, "he's looking through them. As a professor at New York University, he works on Washington Square Park, one of the great public spaces in the world. Any given moment, he is surrounded by hundreds or thousands of people of every race and age, acting and interacting...But none of this, alas, happens in Sennett's city; as far as he is concerned, nothing like this has happened for the last two-hundred years. I picture him trudging through the square, wrapped up in his theory that all modern men are wrapped up in themselves, oblivious to the overflowing life all around him. Too bad, because this public life, as spectacular as ever in the cities of today, can rescue us from our personal sorrows and anxieties, nourish us and renew our strength, help us make it through the day and night...If social theorists want their minds and their world to come to life again, they need to make new friends."

Mike Davis was another urbanist who felt the brunt of Marshall's occasional acerbic pen—his trusty Papermate felt-tipped pen, in assorted colors (pink, purple, and green were personal favorites). Marshall's great review of Davis's great book on Los Angeles, *City of Quartz*, also appeared in *The Nation*: "I said that *City of Quartz* is refreshing in its neglect of Hollywood, but this isn't quite true. There's a full frontal Hollywood in Davis's back-cover self-presentation. He doesn't mention going to school anywhere or studying anything with anyone, so I guess we're meant to think he learned all he knows at the rack or on the road. Above the jacket copy there's an elaborately staged (and stagy) cover photo, in which the author comes on like Charles

Bukowski's doomed younger brother. We see him standing on a closed overpass (evoking factory or prison garb), dressed in proletarian clothes, glaring out at us as if to say this is his turf and he doesn't want company, hugging himself tight to fight off the DTs or maybe the existential cold. The look is that of an ageing, ravaged light-heavyweight who could have been a contender but has taken too many shots to the head."

It was a typical gadflyish Marshall put-down. Rumor out on the street was that ex-meat-cutter, truck-driver tough-guy Davis didn't dig Berman's dig, and would punch him out next time they met. Hadn't anybody told Davis that teddy bear, peace-loving Marshall wouldn't take much punching out! Marshall's review of *City of Quartz* was always an all-time favorite of mine in part because Davis's *City of Quartz* was always an all-time favorite of mine, one of the greatest urban books ever. I remember buying *City of Quartz* when it first came out, thrillingly, at the MoMA bookstore. I was visiting New York from Baltimore; in the latter place I was spending a sandwich year at grad school, at Johns Hopkins, between my stint at Oxford. David Harvey told me I should go to Baltimore, study it, he said; the city once deemed "the armpit of the East" would make a good comparison with Liverpool. David lived and taught in Baltimore for decades prior to moving to Oxford, still kept his house there, near Homewood campus, in Hampden. Part of the house was vacant. He said I could stay there if I wanted. I did want.

When I came to New York that Christmas I got a ride off another grad student with a car. We blasted up Interstate 95 one Friday night in the pouring rain. He dropped me off on the Lower East Side, along Avenue A. For some reason I'll always remember the music playing in the car as we cruised the East Village's dark and wet streets—John Coltrane, his sixteen-minute lead-out number, "Africa," from the 1961 experimental album *Africa/Brass*. Those menacing syncopations of Coltrane's tenor, hooting like frantic car horns, will always remain evocative of that evening, with its wild jungle feel, an unknown chaos, an impending doom, demonic and threatening. Coltrane's sax and the brass section, the drums and piano and bass, all worked against each other, in a disruptive cacophony, perfect for the kinetic sound of the city that evening, any evening, a brilliantly inventive jazz that forever plays in my brain when I think of New York, pulsating with an energy at once scary and invigorating.

To call it scary and invigorating was about right then because the Lower East Side was just that. I stepped out of the car with Tompkins Square Park immediately before me. In those days it was tent city for New York's ever-expanding homeless population, hundreds of residues and displacees of Ed Koch's mayoral years.

Everything was soggy and tense that night. Conditions were gruesome; lots of angry shouting and growling dogs, chained to trees, frothing at the mouth, as well as a heavy-handed police presence, similarly frothing at the mouth, patrolling the perimeter of the twelve-acre park; an odd commingling of Sesame Street, Hooverville and Haight-Ashbury, someone called it. For a while the space had been highly contested terrain. Homeless populations, housing advocates, and East Village anarchists regularly clashed with the NYPD. Local residents were split. Some knew these people had no place else to go, couldn't afford to live anyplace else in town; the city had betrayed them; others wanted them cleared away, out of sight and out of mind.

This stark dystopian backdrop prologued my New York City visit and set the tone of the urban zeitgeist. Mike Davis caught this zeitgeist in *City of Quartz*, gave it a dazzlingly new narrative form. It was his *style* that I'd found so captivating. Davis could really write, had tremendous storytelling gifts. He wove together cultural history and politics, economics and literature, film and music, capturing the whole city, the whole implicate order, while keeping his nose close to the street, pacing the sidewalk, cruising the freeway. A giant city like Los Angeles was laid down solid on the page, in print. This wasn't dry scholarship. It was the real thing, he was the real thing, a gritty urbanist after my own heart, one I wanted to emulate. I even *liked* the stagy flap image of him, hugging himself under an underpass, coming on like Bukowski's doomed younger brother—as Marshall said! There were plenty of places in Baltimore where I could similarly hug myself, affect the same DT pose.

Davis amalgamated all the things a thirty-year-old grad student, struggling to write an academic PhD, could only dream about. I wanted to pull off a similar scam myself, but knew I couldn't. Not as a PhD. I knew it would take me someplace else, someplace beyond academia. I was envious and admiring of Davis in equal measure. He'd blended together *Blade Runner* with Antonio Gramsci, hip-hop gangbangers with Scientologists, critical urban theory with Raymond Chandler; Cal jazz legends Art Pepper and Ornette Coleman shared airtime with novelist Thomas Pynchon. This was a Marxism beyond my wildest fantasies, and I wanted more. It was dramatic and exciting. When Davis spoke about the jazz and literature I loved, his prose soared: "Living in Skid Row hotels, jamming in friends' garages, and studying music theory between floors during his stint as an elevator operator at Bullocks Wilshire, Ornette Coleman was a cultural guerrilla in the Los Angeles of the 1950s." Meanwhile, Art Pepper "studied bebop on Central Avenue, did graduate work on heroin in Boyle Heights, and became emeritus at San Quentin."

As for Thomas Pynchon, his *Crying of Lot 49* (1966) "provided the ultimate freeway-map ontology of Southern California." "As radically 'decentered' as any contemporary Althusserian could have wished, *Crying of Lot 49* wastes no time grappling with the alienation of its subject."

Marshall, of course, was *opinionated* about Mike Davis. The street-fighting, tough guy persona you got from Davis, wasn't really Marshall's shtick. But he'd appreciated how Davis had carried off something special. Davis wrote beautifully, Marshall said, "about less glamorous places and themes of LA's; about its industrial ghost towns, like Fontana, where Davis was born in 1946, full of shattered dreams and awaiting new development." "Fontana probably has more wrecked cars per capita than anywhere else on the planet," Davis said. The town is full of wrecks. "Scattered amid the broken bumper cars and Ferris wheel seats are nostalgic bits and pieces of Southern California's famous extinct amusement parks. Suddenly rearing up from the back of a flatbed trailer are the fabled stone elephants and pouncing lions that once stood at the gates of Selig Zoo in Eastlake (Lincoln) Park, where they had enthralled generations of Eastside kids. I tried to imagine how a native of Manhattan would feel, suddenly discovering the New York Public Library stone lions discarded in a New Jersey wrecking yard. Past generations are like so much debris to be swept away by the developers' bulldozer. In which case it is only appropriate that they should end up here, in Fontana—the junkyard of dreams."

"Narratives like these," Marshall said in his review, "not only show Davis at his best but also, I believe, show Marxism doing what it can do best: bring us closer to the historical long waves that drive and wreck our everyday lives; force us to see ourselves and one another and our whole society and all our inner contradictions in depth face to face. If Marxist thought can do that, I think it has plenty to be proud of." Still, Marshall knew that for some Marxists this isn't enough, never enough. "They feel Marxism has to provide a transcendent revolutionary *zap*. It has to bestow the powers that Jim Morrison pursued—to break on through to the other side, to bring on the end—or else it isn't worth anything."

Marshall's great insight into *City of Quartz* was also an insight, I know now, into myself. I'd shared then, perhaps without even recognizing it, the two souls that dwelled in Mike Davis's own breast. Davis, too, had a yearning for this "Big Bang" zap; a radical concerned citizen, Marshall said, both humane and humanitarian, "who wants to grasp the totality of city life"; and yet he's equally "a radical guerrilla aching to see the whole damned thing blow." Is he embracing the whole city or telling it all to go to hell?

Doubtless he's yearning for both, maybe at the same time. This is perhaps what makes *City of Quartz* so enthralling. "Who will he be, try to be?" Marshall wondered, "Whitman or Céline? Davis sounds unsure, but I'm rooting for Whitman."

Marshall was good for me, Corinna said. He was a generous soul when I sometimes wasn't, a guy who tried to see the good in the bad, seeing positivity beyond negativity. I had a lot of negativity in me, frequently without much positivity. It wasn't like I was a pessimist; I mean, I wasn't. I was angry somehow, an angry optimist, a dark optimist. He was gentle spirit, a hugger rather than a puncher, a man who saw the power of love frustrating the power of hate. He was a partisan of happiness, of joy over misery, a Whitman rather than a Céline. Joy will give people more power to change the world for the better, Marshall said. Alas, I had a lot of hate in me, a periodic desire to fight, to punch people out, to let off steam, to be punched. I was miserable and sometimes enjoyed being miserable.

But in Marshall I saw my shadow self, my better half, the part Corinna thought I should affirm, the fraction she was attracted to. She wanted to love me as a whole number and I wanted to reciprocate. In Mike Davis I recognized my angrier part, the undertow that tugged with my Marshall part, the loving part. These were the two souls dwelling in my breast, dwelling in my feeling and thinking about cities as well. I was more dystopian than utopian. Funnily enough, this is what I wanted to discuss with Marshall. We'd agreed to see each other again, to meet up after French Roast, just the two of us, in a few days' time. I wanted to talk to him about a letter he'd sent me about an article I'd sent him.

Both were about Marx's and Dostoevsky's concept of suffering and freedom and why their concepts might be important for urbanists. It was another way to frame the Whitman and Céline split. Marshall thought it a great idea, told me so in a wonderful letter, handwritten in his handsome cursive, on Gothic sepia notepaper, rimmed by gargoyles and demons, by lions pulling tongues and deformed monkeys looking like crippled humans. It was trippy, little green man notepaper, spookier than you'd imagine coming from Marshall. Maybe this was *his* shadow self on display?

In his letter, Marshall said I should send my article to *Dissent* or *New Left Review*. "It'll look great in print!" he said. I did send it to *Dissent* who quickly passed, and afterward to *New Left Review*, who likewise weren't smitten. They weren't so fast. I'm not sure they ever got back to me. We'll be in touch, they said. Which meant they'd never be back in touch. The routine was getting familiar: *rejection*. But the piece did eventually get placed, or *buried*, in a pointless academic journal nobody read called

Rethinking Marxism. What counted most then was Marshall's affirmative response, that handwritten letter, worth a million referees' reports. "Your Marx-Dost piece immediately disappeared into one of the hundreds of stacks of paper," he'd written me, "and I just retrieved it a couple of days ago. I enjoyed it a lot! I've always looked for a way to juxtapose that 'suffering' passage in M+D, but I've never figured out how. So now I'm both a little envious and a lot relieved—you've done it, weight's off my head."

"One place where you can bed down M+D," Marshall said, "is the desire to overcome mechanical, closed-society models of the good life. M's romance of 'free development' is meant as an alternative to classical and medieval closed societies. Marx enjoyed Utopian thought, ripped it off plenty, and stayed friends with Moses Hess (who may have even written some of the *Manifesto*). But he dissed it because all its models were Crystal Palaces. So you could see M+D both engaged in imagining critical + radical forms of an Open Society." This was vital Marshall, his whole life-spirit there in print, in a preciously handwritten letter, to me, revealing as much about his own model of the good life as "M+D's."

For years, I'd been a huge fan of Dostoevsky's novella from 1864, *Notes from Underground*, even considered myself an Underground Man. The book had kept me going in Liverpool after I'd quit school at sixteen, when I was reluctantly forced to engage with the overground. Dostoevsky spoke about a long-suffering "underground" character. This Underground Man had a "hysterical craving for contrasts and contradictions" and wondered whether human beings liked something else besides prosperity. Maybe, the Underground Man said, we like suffering just as much? Suffering meant doubt, meant negation, and "what would be the good of a Crystal Palace if there could be no doubt about it?"

The Crystal Palace was the Underground Man's allusion to Joseph Paxton's pinnacle structure at London's 1851 Great Exhibition. It was an immense glass and steel building that became the model of Nikolai Chernyshevsky's socialist utopia, descriptions of which form the most radiant passages of his serialized novel, *What Is to Be Done*? Appearing a year before *Notes from Underground*, Dostoevsky hated Chernyshevsky's novel as well as his idea of a Crystal Palace society. Dostoevsky had seen the Crystal Palace himself, the real thing, in 1862, after Paxton's building had moved to Sydenham Hill, and he gasped in awe at the sight of this "monument of ultimate truth," yet recoiled in horror at the thought of living in it. "You feel that something has been achieved here," Dostoevsky said, "that here there is victory and triumph. No matter how independent you might be, for some reason you become terrified." It was, Dostoevsky said, but a facile attempt to apply reason to resolve existential dilemmas.

In the Crystal Palace, there'd be "nothing left to do"; you'd not be able to stick your tongue out at it, Dostoevsky's Underground Man said, nor "thumb your nose on the sly." What worried him most wasn't whether abolishing disorder and conflict was possible but whether it was *desirable*. He hoped people would only love Crystal Palaces "from a distance," invent them as fantasies but not want to inhabit them in reality. For living in them meant the end of novelty, of adventure and fantasy, the end of Mike Davis's dystopian panorama in *City of Quartz*. Everything would become routine, the death knell of the spirit. Passion would be throttled, and from where, Dostoevsky's Underground Man wondered, would intensity of experience, that sole origin of consciousness, then emanate?

I'd said, in my article, that this concern chimed with the young Karl Marx. I knew, when I said it, Marshall would be on my wavelength; perhaps the only person on my wavelength! After all, he'd pioneered the whole frequency in the first place, tuned me into how Marx, in the *Economic and Philosophic Manuscripts of 1844*, framed things strikingly similarly. Like Dostoevsky's, Marx's point of departure was that humans are endowed with "vital powers." Vital powers, Marx said, exist in us as "dispositions," as "capacities" and "drives." We come to know ourselves by passionately using these vital powers to feel and see and comprehend the external world all around us, a world simultaneously ours and one which incorporates other people. Passion, Marx said, is our "essential power vigorously striving to attain its object."

"To be sensuous is to *suffer* (to be subjected to the actions of another)." (The italic is Marx's.) Suffering is an "integral human essence," Marx said, "an enjoyment of the self for man." The Underground Man couldn't agree more! This was Marx affirming the primacy of "free conscious activity" in the "species-character of man," the vitality of free will and individuality—features so dear to Marshall's own heart, to his own species-character. It was why, too, Marx indicted capitalism so ardently; not simply because it makes people suffer—of course it makes people suffer—but that it makes people suffer in a particularly crippling manner. The senses are numbed rather than stimulated; the parameters of free individual development are restricted, despite what capitalists say about freedom. Marx, like Marshall, yearned for a society where people fully express their individualities and desires. Both men were into *positive* suffering, wanted a society where each human sense—seeing, hearing, smelling, tasting, feeling, thinking, contemplating, sensing, acting, loving (the list is Marx's)—could blossom as "organs of individuality," become "theoreticians in their immediate praxis."

When we suffer we feel, we learn things about ourselves intellect alone can't discern. It's a learning process, "an integral human essence." It happens to everybody, everywhere, at all times, whether we like it or not, whether we confront it or not, acknowledge it or not. Strangely, we need it somehow. Painful encounters offer an intensity of experience that help us become *whole* people; paradoxically it may even make us feel, in Dostoevsky's language, "*more alive*," helping us stave off what Marx called "one-sided individuality." All told, it seems, we, as human beings, crave a society where both positive and negative passions need to get played out and worked through, openly and honestly, and here the city comes into its own, makes its life-form so compelling as a life-force. Because there, and maybe only there, could people vigorously strive to attain their object. So it was like Marshall said in his letter: Marx and Dostoevsky—or M+D—are existential bedfellows. They challenge us to imagine critical and radical forms of an Open Society.

I'd met Marshall at Starbucks on West 71st Street, near the Lincoln Center. His choice again, a curious one given all he'd said about critical and radical forms of an Open Society. Didn't Starbucks epitomize uniformity and alienation? Wasn't it the scourge of independent coffee shops? Manhattan alone has over a hundred and fifty Starbucks, seemingly one on every other corner of the Upper West Side. They all looked the same, smelled the same, had that same metallic bitterness to the coffee. Employees seemed disconnected from anything, including themselves, comatosed as they took your order, which they frequently got wrong. Pay was lousy. Tables were littered with customer debris, infrequently cleaned up. Each store felt scummy, uncared for. Toilets were filthy, more often broken and out of order. Spawning throughout New York, Starbucks spread like a contagious disease.

But Marshall didn't see it that way. He saw other things happening in Starbucks, other dialectical things. Above all, Starbucks were places where people encountered other people, dated other people, fell in love with other people. He didn't care two hoots about the coffee or about the toilets or about the labor practices or about monopolization. All that was surface. Starbucks were open all-hours meaning people could schmooze all-hours, hang out all-hours, overcome alienation through intense human contact, human proximity, potential intimacy; even sitting in front of your laptop, tapping away at your keyboard, next to someone, not talking to anyone, you were embracing other people, a stranger engaged in strange communication. Marshall saw people in Starbucks as a public remaking the private, doing it together, as a collectivity, reappropriating the corporate through an agglomeration of the civic. That's how his modernist brain worked. It was a human thing for him, people becoming "ripe." "Ripeness was all," Edgar said in *King Lear*. Marshall loved this line. New York was full of people trying to become ripe, and Starbucks, for him, was one place as fruitful as any other.

Besides, he told me there was a personal reason why he liked Starbucks, this one in particular: it was the venue of his first date with future wife Shellie, who works around the corner, at the Professional Children's School, a school for kids gifted in the performing arts, a sort of "Fame" school, where she teaches English literature and drama. This Starbucks played a role for them much as the Dôme in Covent Garden played for Corinna and me: *it was where it all began*. How could anybody *not* have a soft spot for someplace where you fell in love? I guess Marshall thought plenty of people fell in love in Starbucks. He'd met me here today, too, because it was convenient. He'd just seen his shrink, he said, whose practice was nearby. Marshall had no qualms telling me about seeing his shrink. He'd been seeing him for a long while, been in therapy on and off since the "murder" of his son Marc. Later this afternoon, he said, he had a parents' meeting at Eli's school, his eldest son from a previous marriage. The school was close by. Marshall said Meredith, his ex, would stop by in a while, so he'd look out for her and I could say hi.

He was lively that afternoon, alert and upbeat. Maybe a bit anxious, too, with a lot of nervous energy flowing through him, after seeing his shrink, anticipating meeting his ex. I remember he spoke about a "classic form of suffering without injustice": *unrequited love*. Marshall told me he'd always wanted to write a book about romantic love. It would be about love both fulfilled and unfulfilled, he said, about "archetypal couples" in the "history of modern culture," like Romeo and Juliet, like Papageno and Papagena from Mozart's *The Magic Flute*. "Maybe stories of love crushed are more poignant than stories of love fulfilled," he said. "Or maybe the best story is love crushed *after* it's fulfilled." It was right out of Carver, like Ed's cruel fate in "What We Talk About When We Talk About Love." What kind of suffering leads a man to swallow rat poison or to try to blow his brains out? What kind of love forces somebody to want to kill a loved one, to drag them by their hair? "People are different, Mel," Carver had Terri say. "Sure, sometimes Ed may have acted crazy. Okay. But he loved me. In his own way maybe, but he loved me. There was love there, Mel. Don't say there wasn't."

Marshall said the young Marx acknowledged unrequited love in his 1840s writings. I should check them out, add a section or two in my article. This seemed important to Marshall. It'd been important to Marx, Marshall said. Marx was a product of his generation, heavily influenced, like everybody else then, by Goethe. Marx enjoyed Goethean thought. Those youthful essays from the 1840s have plenty of *Sturm und Drang* in them, Marshall said. In the *Economic and Philosophic Manuscripts*, Marx wrote: "If you love without evoking love in return—if through the vital expression of yourself as a loving person you fail to become a loved person, then your love is impotent, a misfortune." Here's another Marx line, this time from *The Holy Family* (1845), where love got affirmed over "critical criticism": "What critical criticism fights against here is not merely love but everything living. Love really teaches a man to believe in the objective world outside himself. It not only makes man the object but the object a man. Love makes the beloved into an external object, a sensuous object which does not remain internal, hidden in the brain."

One of the great works of unrequited love was *The Sorrows of the Young Werther* (1774), Goethe's tale of a "misfortunate" twenty-something. The bond between the melancholy Werther and Marx's entourage of Young Hegelians, twenty-something philosophers wearing frock coats and smart breeches, suffering from unrequited love affairs, is perhaps tight. "The question," Werther said, "isn't whether a man is strong or weak, but whether he is able to endure the measure of his sufferings?" Dumbfounded, impotent in love, Werther throws in the towel, querying the heavens:

"Must it ever be thus that the source of our happiness must also be the fountain of our misery?"

The other great tale of unrequited love on Marshall's radar was Bazarov's, the would-be nihilist of Turgenev's *Fathers and Children* (1862). Bazarov wanted to negate everything, clear away everything. He scoffed at the saccharine romantics of his father's generation. But when Bazarov encountered love, his powers of negativity failed him. He was beloved to an external object, to a positive force that eventually destroyed him, a source of happiness that became the fountain of misery. At first, talking to the enigmatic aristocratic Anna Sergeyevna, Bazarov voiced "frigid scorn for everything romantic." But soon love's spell began to work even on him; "left alone he was brought indignantly face to face with the romantic in himself." He'd set off into the forest, walking through it with great strides, "snapping off branches which came in his way and swearing *sotto voce* at both her and himself."

And then, in one of Turgenev's most tumultuous scenes, passion erupts. Bazarov stood with his back to Anna, mumbling: "Well you might as well know, then, that I love you—stupidly beyond all reason. There, now you have what you have been angling for." Anna "held out both her hands to him, but Bazarov pressed his forehead against the window pane. He was fighting for breath; his whole body was shaking visibly. But it was no trembling of youthful shyness, no sweet awe of a first declaration, which had taken possession of him: it was passion that throbbed in him, heavy and potent—a passion not unlike anger, and perhaps akin to it." Anna "felt a mounting fear of him—and pity." Bazarov turned around, "devoured her with one eager look and seizing both her hands suddenly pulled her against his chest. She did not at once free herself from his embrace but a moment later she was standing well away in a corner regarding Bazarov from across the room. He lunged toward her. '*You misunderstood me*,' she whispered with hasty fear."

It was the *coup de grâce*, the beginning of Bazarov's end. No iron could have more effectively entered his soul than that *you misunderstood me*. It's hard to imagine who hasn't been *there*. I think the first time I really experienced unrequited love, remember being hurt by it, was in my late teens. Her name was Paula. We sort of met in a Woolton pub. It was a Saturday night, a sort of meeting because I only stood next to her. That was close enough. I smelled her, heard her, watched her, immediately idolized her, yet never spoke to her. I merely watched somebody I knew talk to her. That was how I found out her name. I quizzed the person later, probed him for information. Where did she live? What did she do? How old was she? Did she have a boyfriend? What was her favorite color? I constructed an imaginary profile.

She was about my age, slim, of medium height, with short, sandy-colored hair. Fetching rather than beautiful. There was an elfin magnetism about her, something I'd later see in Corinna. She was a regular at the pub so I became a regular at the pub. She stood there with her boyfriend, also a regular at the pub, also her regular boyfriend. I stood close by, ogling, looking at Paula, at her dress and dark stockings, slipping her shoes on and off. I liked that, liked that a lot. I was rough, had spotty skin, crooked teeth, was introverted, self-conscious and insecure, had no car, no money, no education, no prospects. Hardly a catch. She was a hairdresser, went for flash guys, with cars, with money. It was hopeless. But I wasn't deterred. I finally spoke to her. She asked my name, what I did. I remember I was a stammering wreck. My brain and mouth lost their unity, my pulse raced, legs quivered. I was on fire, glowing red, dying on the spot.

Paula was all composure, confident, fresh-faced, had shiny hair, perfect skin and teeth, was chirpy and frivolous. Nothing seemed to worry her. Life was fine. She was so happy she never thought about happiness. I was tense and angry, unhappy. We weren't exactly well-matched. My behavior was compulsive. I had flowers sent to her house. She avoided going to the pub that week, I recall. I was there. She wasn't. I'd been snubbed. Then I wrote to the local radio station, Radio Merseyside, with a request: "To Paula from Andy, the guy in the pub who likes you and wants to know you better." Something like that. It was trite even to call it trite. Worse was to come. The dedication: Stevie Wonder's "You Are the Sunshine of My Life." I could never listen to that song again, still can't. Paula wasn't impressed. You're a sweet guy, Andy, and I'm really flattered, but... *You misunderstood me.* I sought advice from an honest friend. Give it up, mate, he said, forget it. I did forget it, eventually, of course. But love comes around, and around.

Marshall championed love fulfilled winning out against all odds. "One human right that seems to embarrass academic and political writers," he wrote in 2010, in a new afterword to *All That Is Solid Melts into Air*, "is *the right to love.*" "Love isn't just an accessory of meaning; it is central to what human life can mean," Marshall said. That's a pretty beautiful thought. Love blooms where it will, Marshall said. It can be painful and tragic but sometimes, "Papageno and Papagena overcome: you see them together on Saturdays, shopping in markets and malls, exhausted but radiant, with strollers and kids in colors never known to man." Papageno and Papagena, Marshall said, confronted "the dragons of a malevolent state that tried to destroy their life together. The *Loving* complex of ideas may soon become the constitutional basis for gay marriage. If that happens, it will be a great victory for the right to love."

Marshall told me he'd had a couple of failed marriages before meeting Shellie. He'd wedded Meredith Tax, his second wife, in 1982. She was a writer, he said, wrote some pretty good historical fiction like *Rivington Street*, about Hannah Levy, a courageous Jewish matriarch at the turn of the century, living on the Lower East Side; and *Union Square*, its sequel, set in the interwar Jazz Age. Perhaps more important, though, were her historical nonfiction books on the women's movement, like *Rising of the Women*. She's still active in feminist issues. We were in love for a while but it faded, Marshall said. She thought I was cramping her style, he said, crushing her own creativity; two writers in the same apartment was one too many for her. They had a kid together, Eli, born in 1984.

Marshall got a little agitated talking about Meredith, and at the thought that soon she'd be here. I wasn't quite sure where I stood. I'd just be polite, I guess, recede into background. I was only getting to know Marshall anyway. But then he spotted Meredith outside on the sidewalk, about to enter. She'll come over and say hello, he said. She was a short, plumpish woman with a shock of curly red hair, wearing sunglasses. Marshall tried to grab another chair, making space for her to sit, and struggled to raise himself from his seat to greet her. But upon entering, Meredith suddenly turned her head away from him, turned it up and to the side, in a kind of deliberate, haughty snub, and proceeded to stroll right by him, right through him really, ignoring him and me, not saying a word as Marshall stood there, holding out his arms. It was stunningly painful, embarrassing to watch him. I think he felt humiliated in front of me. I wished I hadn't seen it, been there to see it. He turned around to me, bewildered, literally speechless for a few seconds. "*Oy!*" he said, finally, shaking his head in disbelief, looking at me pitifully, "*Oy!*"

In ***The Brothers Karamazov,*** Dostoevsky said there's nothing more wholesome in life than a good memory, especially a good memory from childhood. This memory not only sustains you in the present, he said, but also helps propel you into the future. People talk about how important education is; but some sacred memory, preserved from childhood, is, for Dostoevsky, the best education of all. If you can keep hold of it into adulthood, "you're safe till the end of your days."

The older I get, the more that childhood image atop the Empire State remains primal. It's one of the few strong memories I guard from childhood. As time passes, it's hard to know if this memory becomes more vivid because it's preserved, or if its reality is a reinvention of my adult imagination, a wishful construction rather than a factual reconstruction. Before this memory, there's little else. My only other positive memory is going to the eye hospital with my mother. I must have been about seven or eight years old. It happened a few times a year and lasted several years. Before going to America, I think those trips to St. Paul's eye hospital in Liverpool were the thrill of my life. I'll never forget them, even though they're gone forever and that makes me sad. But I can always conjure up the image of those journeys with my mother, going on the bus into "town."

Since I was very young my eyes were bad. My mother reckoned it was due to the fall I had when I cracked the side of my head on the fireplace. Thereafter I developed a squint in my right eye. Glasses were prescribed and so began a kind of disability and torture. But there were advantages. After all, I got to make trips to the hospital with my mother. I remember going there, squeezing her hand as we'd walk across Exchange Flags, behind the Town Hall. I can still feel that feeling, the feeling of squeezing hands. Everything seemed bustling and exciting then; downtown Liverpool was so full of people; the buildings seemed to shine. I was a happy child during the mid-1960s, before Liverpool began to decline, before people began to leave, before the buildings became shabby and forlorn. That was the 1970s, when I became an unhappy child, a melancholy child—a moon child my mother called me. But just then, in the mid-1960s, as a kid, Liverpool's city center was the greatest place on earth, such a big adventure going there.

We had a set routine throughout those years. In the hospital, we'd go up a windy staircase where the eye doctor had his machine. I'd put my chin on its little shelf and look at pictures of all kinds of animals: horses, cats, dogs, and rabbits. I had to move a lever, try to place each animal into a cage, or take them out of their cages, or line each animal up. I didn't know what this was all about but I knew it was a whole lot of fun. My mother would be there, too, encouraging me, laughing at her young son whose eyesight was bad and who had on these big milk-bottle glasses. Maybe she guessed I was shy and afraid that I might have to stay in hospital for a while.

But the real treat came afterward. Then, my mother would take me out to eat. We so rarely ate out that it was always special. We'd stop off each time at the Indian restaurant above Hobbies, a kids' toy store I loved, long gone, along with the restaurant. My mother used to let me have chicken curry. As ever, she knew it would be way too hot. I don't know why I had it because each time she'd have to ask for more water to cool my mouth down. We'd laugh about it as I'd sweat and suffer, gasping for air, fanning my mouth. I know now the curry probably wasn't very good. Yet for me right there and then it was the best curry in the whole world. This was the city of my childhood. Maybe it's just an imaginary vision, an invented memory of ghosts, conjured up in my head on the basis of feeling, the feeling of a self and a city that is no more, a little boy and his city disappearing into the fog of lost time.

The other vivid memory I have from childhood is less positive. It still haunts me. Here, too, as I get older, I wonder how much this memory has shaped my life. I must have been a bit younger than ten. We were on vacation, me, my sister, my mother and father, in North Wales, at the Butlin's holiday camp in Pwllheli. I would have been really excited, and remember after we'd checked into our first-floor room—it's hard for me to imagine how cheap and basic this room must have been—I bounded out onto the exterior balcony, legging up and down. Butlin's had rows and rows of uniform blocks, each floor with its own external balcony, unadorned motel-like dorms, affordable holiday accommodation for modest-means families like mine. I was thrilled to be on vacation, away from home, out of school for the summer, beside the sea, with all sorts of fun amusements, like bumper cars and little steam train rides.

Then something awful occurred. It doesn't sound awful today but it was then. I remember running back into our room, literally bursting through the door, knowing I'd cause my mother and father and sister to stir. The problem was I burst back into the *wrong* room, somebody else's, a room with the exact same features, yet not ours. Next door's, or next door's but one. I'm not sure. All I knew was that, for a brief instant, I was horrified by the sight of people I didn't recognize, another family, other faces, unfamiliar faces, unknown people. They were almost as shocked as I was, having been burst into, an unexpected guest storming in. I nearly screamed, but managed to turn around, and run out panic-stricken, wondering if I'd ever find the right room again, where my mum and dad and sister were. By the time I was outside, I saw my father on balcony, looking for me. I never mentioned anything to him, never mentioned the incident to anybody, not ever.

I can still remember that shock feeling, glimpsing another family in what I thought was our room; strange faces, intruders in the midst. How this has affected me into adulthood I cannot be certain. But it has affected me somehow. I'm suspicious of people, guarded and untrusting, prone to retreat into my shell if I feel threatened, living up to my birth sign, the most defensive in the Zodiac. But perhaps it also has something to do with that incident. My primal instinct ever since is to be defensive, to run for cover, unless otherwise reassured. It's a personal default position that seldom gives people an *a priori* benefit of the doubt.

In adulthood, I've had to work hard to overcome this defensive instinct. Corinna said I'd be better off, happier, if I did overcome it. I knew it was very *un*Marshall-like, the direct opposite to his philosophy of life. Marshall opened himself up to trouble, tried to strip away his inner defenses, like Allen Ginsberg taking his clothes off in a 1960s be-in, expressing authenticity through nakedness, exposing himself, converting emotional honesty into immense vulnerability. A good thing! This sensibility was evoked in a review Marshall once wrote of a collection of Isaac Bashevis Singer's short stories. One Singer tale, "The Key," Marshall said, holds the key—the key to Marshall's (and Singer's) feelings about people, feelings about the neighborhood, the Upper West Side, where the story is set. It was the 1960s, when people, especially lone people, had every reason to fear other people on the street. The story's heroine, Bessie Popkin, an old Singer lady, mixes her fear of the street with a loathing of street people. Her fear and loathing soon becomes a "paranoid eruption," Marshall said, a hatred of going out, of having to shop, of encountering others. One summer afternoon, she's coming home from Broadway, laden with heavy shopping bags. She puts her key in her apartment lock and turns it, "but woe," Singer wrote, "the key broke. Only the handle remained in her hand. Bessie fully grasped the catastrophe."

She has nowhere to turn. She goes back onto Broadway, looking for a locksmith. But none are open. Then she sits down on a bench, on Broadway Mall, the green strip splitting Broadway between Columbus Circle and 122nd Street, and dozes off. She awakens with a start. It's already daybreak. From the side of Central Park the sun rises. The sky above Broadway becomes pink and reddish; flames kindle windowpanes. A pigeon lands nearby. She inhales the moist morning air, smelling of grass and coffee. People bustle past her, going to work, buying newspapers, disappearing down into the subway. They're silent and peaceful. This morning Bessie feels cleansed. She even smiles at people; they return the smile, bid her good morning. She reaches her building anxious at having to ask her superintendent for help. But he's sympathetic, actually nice: "Why didn't you come to me and tell me what happened? To be roaming around all night at your age—my God." And her neighbor helped, too, took in the shopping bags Bessie left outside the door, putting the milk and butter in her fridge. "Oh, my good people," Bessie says, barely holding back her tears.

"Ironically," said Marshall, "we know it is only through *roaming around* that Bessie started to become human again," human enough to trust people, to ask for help. "'The Key' may be the sweetest story Singer ever wrote," Marshall said. It's about "letting loose the bitterness that the writer is trying to transcend. The spleen and bile flood in at the story's start: 'hordes of urchins, a mob of thieves, robbers and whores'. But Singer empowers his heroine to overcome fear and loathing and reach a point where she can be here and now and share space with the rest of the people of the Upper West Side—and of the earth—and live with them. That's the key."

At the end of the tale, Bessie lies down on her bed and reminisces about her late husband Sam, remembering their honeymoon in the Catskills. They were led by the hotel owner to the bridal suite, and he said to them, in the same voice and intonation as the superintendent: "You don't need no key here. Just enter—and *mazel tov*."

The Empire State Building was my Empire State of the mind, something loving for me, thrilling and joy-giving. So it was there where I wanted to propose to Corinna. I tipped her off it might happen during this trip, downplayed it, because I felt embarrassed. I think I felt embarrassed because I didn't think I was the marrying type. I had no real idea what the marrying type meant. But I suppose deep down I felt I was a loner, somebody who had always expected to be single, on their own. The few people who knew me well thought that, too. They were surprised that now I was with someone, a person with whom I could be happy, counteracting what many anticipated—including myself:

preordained unhappiness. Now, maybe, happiness was a real-life concept, a possibility, being a husband, the lesser half of a couple. Maybe I was as freaked by the prospect of marriage as Spalding Gray had been. I needed to let out a howl.

I'd intimated it to Corinna—marriage, that is—that we should do it here, consecrate it in the city I loved, with the person I loved, up a building I loved. It was one of those cherished Dostoevskian moments of real education, the memory of a ten-year-old boy on top of the world, in every sense. This proposal plan had been on my mind when I'd met Marshall; I may have even mentioned it to him. Though the incident with his ex shook me. I felt for him; felt for myself. Will this love I knew last? How to explain Meredith's behavior? She really seemed to hate Marshall's guts, in true Carveresque style. It was hard to conceive how anybody could hate Marshall.

Corinna grimaced when I'd told her about the incident in Starbucks. Poor Marshall. When he and I were together she'd had a wonderful time on her own, exploring her favorite place on the entire earth: Zabar's, the legendary Upper West Side food store, at Broadway and 80th Street. Corinna loved the ground-floor food counters, loved strolling around the prepared foods in the aisles, eyeing everything under the sun, sampling each freebie. But her real passion wasn't downstairs but upstairs, in the cookware section, with the pots and pans and kitchen utensils, the scales and garlic crushers, the knives and peelers and obscure cooking equipment few people downstairs probably used. New Yorkers weren't really cooks; few actually cooked at home; fewer still had dining tables in their apartments. It was a takeout/dine-out culture. Though Corinna assumed *some* New Yorkers must prepare food at home, cook sometimes, given Zabar's upstairs was so brilliantly stocked.

Corinna never bought prepared foodstuffs, not even sauces, not ever. She'd been schooled by her mother into making *everything* from scratch. So upstairs at Zabar's was like being in heaven for her. She'd spend her spare time rooting around seeing what's what, hunting out bargains, the stuff she needed. We both loved Zabar's next door café, too, and arranged to meet there after I'd seen Marshall. It was an old Upper West Side institution, crammed and cramped with people; the décor and the people were dishevelled, on the older side of life, a bit broken down; nothing fancy, no thrills, and famously brusque service. You lined up, waited with everybody else, bawled out your order nearing the till. You sat where you could, often *very near* somebody. You had to get over personal space issues, talk back if you were talked to, often to some old bag-lady who'd been sitting in Zabar's café for the better part of her life.

You got the sense few here ever ventured beyond the Upper West Side, outcasts and eccentrics, the *dramatis personae* of an I. B. Singer yarn. They were Marshall's people. The green lentil roll was always a great delight for us. I'd eat a lot of them over the years, with a pecan slice for desert. Afterward, I'd browse the book stalls directly outside, on the sidewalk, a guy with medical sunglasses peddling oldies and newies, review copy hardbacks, goodies usually. Philip Roth was a perennial hit. Then I'd wander across Broadway, to Westsider Books, each time marveling that this used bookstore still survived, was there, afloat; a minor miracle as those big chain stores—Staples, Starbucks, Victoria's Secret, Verizon, CVS, Rite Aid, Dunkin' Donuts, McDonald's, Barnes and Noble, etc., etc.—encroached.

That evening we were going up the Empire State Building and that evening was meant to be *the* evening. Yet it was weird. It was a beautiful dry night, crystal clear visibility up on the 86th floor observation deck. A galaxy of twinkling lights enveloped us; we felt part of this vast implicate order, happy to let its gravity suck us into its electrically charged whirlpool. There were many couples there that night, similarly awestruck, likewise in love. We'd even dressed up: I with a tie and dress jacket; Corinna in a dress, looking fabulous. It was something out of Fitzgerald's "My Lost City": "New York had all the iridescence of the beginning of the world." It *was* the beginning of the world for us. And yet, for some inexplicable reason—one of love's great mysteries—I couldn't go through with it, was unable to pull it off. I was so entranced and happy to be there, fully present in the moment, that the words wouldn't come out of my mouth. I passed it up; Corinna was bemused yet said nothing.

It was several days on when I did go through with it. Again we were smartly dressed, kitted out for the occasion, at the roof bar, Salon de Ning; faux Art Deco Shanghai brought to Midtown Manhattan, twenty-odd stories up the Peninsula Hotel, on Fifth Avenue and East 55th Street. In many ways the view was as spectacular as atop the Empire State Building; you could almost touch the Midtown skyline; you were part of it, embedded in it, as you nibbled peanuts and drank Manhattans. It had become our cocktail: bourbon, sweet red vermouth, and a dash of bitters, stirred over ice, strained into a chilled cocktail glass, and garnished with a Maraschino cherry. Perfect. We blasted a small fortune getting tipsy, amongst rich carousing businessmen, who did it every night. We were rich beyond wealth that night, rich beyond earthly riches; and she ACCEPTED.

I remember telling Corinna the only thing I didn't like—hated, in fact—was the monstrosity that towered over us, there almost an arm's length away: 550 Madison Avenue, the Philip

Johnson skyscraper with the "Chippendale top." Known then as the AT&T Building, and later the Sony Tower, its upward sloping roof pediment was modeled on a piece of furniture by Thomas Chippendale, the eighteenth-century English designer. I thought it an awful building and its architect a truly awful man. Built in 1984, the structure was touted as the centerpiece of "postmodernism," created by somebody once a doyen of high-modernism, one of America's best-known twentieth-century architects. *The Village Voice*'s Michael Sorkin hated Johnson's unprincipled approach to architecture, forever fawning to his rich conservative benefactors. Johnson had a crass sense of style, Sorkin said. Throughout the 1980s, Sorkin became Johnson's nemesis, unearthing his pro-Nazi past, his closet antisemitism, his nastiness and ruthless ambition. Johnson later refused to partake in any architectural panel that would include Sorkin; to which Marshall added, laced with irony, that this would be Sorkin's lasting claim to fame.

Philip Johnson cropped up in my life years later, vicariously. In New York, I befriended an architectural critic, Herbert Muschamp, who wrote for *The New York Times*. Herbert, like Marshall, was one of our most exciting and original commentators on buildings and cities. He blended Freud, Marx, Buddhism, and much else in a journalism we'll never see the like again, certainly never in the pages of *The New York Times*. Herbert died of lung cancer in 2007, aged fifty-nine; a big loss for progressive American urbanism. Herbert sparred with Philip Johnson. Herbert also sparred with me for a while, because I once booed him.

I'd booed Herbert in my book *Dialectical Urbanism*. I'd taken offense at a reference he'd made to Guy Debord, the late French urbanist, poet, and filmmaker, in a piece about Times Square in the *Times*'s Sunday magazine. I'd said something like "Muschamp invokes Debord's spectacle but then makes a spectacle out of Debord. Muschamp admires Debord's questioning, postures with Debord's radical criticism, but then flees from Debord's real radicalism, backs away from Debord's politics. Debord saw Muschamp's type coming way back; he would have hated both Muschamp and the new Times Square, would have wanted no part in their show biz, celebrity shallowness." Upon reflection I was a bit aggressive. I was like that back then.

But Herbert didn't mind. He saw my booing as "negative attachment," an invitation to call me up and say, "Hi, there!" Which was pretty much what he did. Herbert said that when I talked about cities I talked from a standpoint the psychoanalyst Melanie Klein called "the depressive position," a love-hate stance, loving one moment, hating the next; sometimes doing both at the same time—you know, like loving to hate. The intensity of the attachment was more evident in the passion of the attack. So it went with my attachment with the city. Herbert was probably right. Our mutual *amour fou*, he recognized, was the city, "the courting ground of crazy love."

I grew to admire what Herbert wrote and said about cities. So I once asked him, half in jest, if he would preface one of my books on the prominent French urban talker, Henri Lefebvre, whose work I knew that Herbert knew. It was such a silly request that Herbert couldn't resist it, saying yes, he would, and he did. It was a weird piece even for a characteristically weird Herbert Muschamp, called "Something Cool." And there he wrote a few revealing words about Philip Johnson. Herbert loved architecture, loved some buildings, often despaired about New York's buildings, even as he loved New York itself, his adopted home town, where as a gay man he found refuge; he loathed its fake pre-modern architecture. Manhattan, he said, is an island within an island, imagining itself to be a leader of Blue State (liberal, Democratic) sensibilities; the record strongly indicated the reverse. It was New York, Herbert said, that brought us Rudy Giuliani's hostility to the First Amendment, zero-tolerance policing initiatives, as well as Donald Trump.

Herbert never saw buildings as autonomous works of art. They were bits and pieces of the city, slotted into the social and political fabric, building blocks of human space, of cities for people. Philip Johnson upheld something else, a rarefied brand of formalism promoted by MoMA. Indeed, he played a vital role ensuring this brand became *the* brand of New York architecture. Buildings were cut off from anything social, anything political, sometimes quite literally. They were there to make land pay; and Johnson's architecture gave bottom-line economics its sheen. Herbert said Johnson always dismissed his architectural criticism, claiming Muschamp's writing "isn't about architecture, of course." Herbert had written this in his preface to my Lefebvre book. The last two words, he'd said, carried the burden of Johnson's meaning. The subject was closed for discussion. That was how Johnson was. Architecture, for Johnson, was the moving and shaping of geometric forms in two and three dimensions. Everything else was sociology, a waste of time.

When we came down to Manhattan street level again, after our Peninsula rooftop escapade, we took a cab to Chelsea, to celebrate at one of my favorite restaurants back then, El Quijote, on the ground floor of the Chelsea Hotel. It wasn't that the food was so great; I just loved the seedy feel of El Quijote, its faded majesty, the hearty portions of its Spanish comfort food—soggy paellas, greasy tapas, and bloated seafood. White tablecloths gave everything a formal air; its waiters dressed like aging, spent bullfighters. I loved El Quijote's black and white checkered floor and the wonderful red mural, dating from the 1930s, with its windmills that namesake Don had jousted, mistaking them for vicious giants. El Quijote's original owners came to America as refugees from Spain, taking over at a peppercorn rent what used to be the Chelsea Hotel's house restaurant. Ever since, El Quijote had survived Chelsea's ever-inflating rents. We gorged on oysters that night, on lobster tails stuffed with crab, on piles of fries, supping it all down with cheap Rioja Blanco. It was an antiquated, overpriced, super-sized affair, a meal locked in a time warp; but we both loved being locked into an older chivalrous time-warp. Tourist trap, we knew; yet two happy trapped tourists we were that special night.

Next Halloween, we got married at Islington Registry Office. It rained all day. We didn't care one bit. I had on a brown tweed suit bought from an Upper Street charity shop, with a purple and yellow silk tie, purchased for eight dollars from a Lower East Side street vendor. Corinna wore a striking pink Vivienne Westwood dress, hugging her petite frame, looking like she'd been born in it. An old school chum read out Walt Whitman's "Song of the Open Road"; it was our song, somewhat adapted and adopted, Corinna's and mine, always would be:

> Afoot and light-hearted we take to the open road,
> Healthy, free, the world before us,
> The road before us leading wherever we choose.

Strong and content we travel the open road.
They go! they go! We know that they go, but we know not where they go,
But we know that they go toward the best—toward something great.

Camerado, I give you my hand!
I give you my love more precious than money,
I give you myself before preaching or law;
Will you give me yourself? will you come travel with me?
Shall we stick by each other as long as we live?

We had a party afterward at the Institute of Contemporary Arts (ICA). Despite its splendor, it was the best-valued marriage venue we could find, majestically overlooking the Mall, near Buckingham Palace. After the meal, guests strayed onto the outside balcony; St. James's Park looked romantic lit up in the mist. It poured down relentlessly, making everything even more atmospheric. The rain was aglow. A jazz quintet riffed. We danced to "This Guy's in Love with You." I kissed Corinna, shuffled as best I could. Holding hands, we pledged forever the excitement and wonder of marriage, of our right to be a couple.

We spent the night in the Covent Garden Hotel, in a room with an enormous bed. When we checked in late afternoon we could hear bebop ringing out beneath us. It took a while to realize we were directly above Ray's Jazz Shop, along Shaftesbury Avenue, where I bought most of my albums. Ray Smith, its owner, had been there since 1975, clinging on in a gentrifying Covent Garden. (In the early 2000s, Ray retired, sold up to Foyles, who immortalized the late Ray—he died in 2011—at the record department of their revamped Charing Cross Road bookstore.)

The following morning, going down for breakfast, the occupant next door, a middle-aged man, was likewise exiting. With well-coiffed, almost-white hair, neatly trimmed gray beard, again almost white, and pale eyes set against a dark complexion, he was instantly recognizable. It was Michael Ondaatje, author of *The English Patient*, who nodded to us. We nodded back, barely holding back our laughter. Corinna and I looked at each other, smiled, shook our heads in disbelief, and thought of John Berger, laughing to ourselves later, laughing out loud. Poor old John...

The depressive position sees a coming together of good and bad objects, of love-hate impulses. This isn't only a "normal enough" developmental stage of any infant—as psychoanalysts say—it's also a normal enough impulse of any critical urbanist. It manifests itself as a peculiarly ambivalent connection to the city, pro-urban yet anti-capitalist. Marx's own feelings about capitalism were ambivalent. He hated capitalism but saw how it brought immense material benefits. Marx wanted these benefits spread about to everybody, available to everyone, not just to a select few, to a ruling class, who monopolized those benefits.

Some people think that after the Berlin Wall collapsed in 1989, and Eastern Bloc governments crumbled, Marx shouldn't be taught anymore, that his thought is obsolete. I remember Marshall saying that American universities today work under a market system and taught what students wanted to learn. Plenty still want to read Marx, he said, because Marx is a thinker who can lead them though the contradictions of capitalism. Those contradictions are most glaring in the city, where capital and wealth accumulates and capitalism expands. Yet cities are also places where people come together en masse to threaten capitalism, to transform it as they somehow transform each other.

So urban talkers like Marshall, like Herbert Muschamp, like Jane Jacobs, denounced the unfair plenty of the capitalist city while they upheld the liberating virtues of urban life. Each writer is positive and negative at the same time. They plunged into the paradoxes of modern urban life and developed individual and collective ways to inhabit a contradictory meantime, where two souls inevitably dwelled within their breasts. They knew, one way or another, a lot about the big city dialectic, about how this dialectic shapes the form and functioning of the city, and how it shapes the form and functioning of any understanding of the city, of any consciousness about the city, its love and hate, the depressive position made happy.

It's a dialectic that recognizes urban shadows, knows that life for many poor urban dwellers is lived in Plato's cave, dark and scary, poverty stricken and dire, spent staring at phantoms. On the other hand, this dialectic also acknowledges the coexistence of light outside the cave, so bright, in fact, that it dazzles your eyes, makes them ache from its brilliance. It's an urban brilliance that promises enormous freedom, ensures radiant shops and enticing goods and services, night clubs catering for every taste and fantasy. Good things under capitalism are inextricably linked to bad things, and that the good life has a nasty habit of turning into the bad life. Under capitalism, Marx said, "everything is pregnant with its contrary." Bad things are the seeds of good things. So, too, with the capitalist city. That's what we talk about when we talk about cities (and sometimes about love).

After our marriage, Corinna and I spent three months in one of the most fascinating and deplored cities on the planet: Los Angeles. But beauty is in the eye of the beholder. Someplace over winter warm and sunny and new to us both was truly glorious. We saw primary colors again, felt heat, could wander about in the daytime in shirtsleeves, sit outside, bask in luscious late afternoon light. This was the first and only sabbatical leave I'd get as an academic. I had a semester as a visiting scholar at UCLA. LA was a blast. Something the old urbanist Henri Lefebvre said about LA stuck in my head: "It's extremely difficult to give an answer to the question of which city one likes and dislikes," he said, "for detestable cities are intriguing. Take Los Angeles. For a European it's appalling and unliveable. You can't get around without a car and you pay exorbitant sums to park it. What fascinates and disgusts me are the streets of luxury shops with superb windows but which you can't enter into. The streets are empty. And not far from here, you have a street, a neighbourhood, where two hundred thousand Salvadoran immigrants are exploited to death in cellars and lofts." Yet there's "singing and dancing," Lefebvre said, "something stupendous and fascinating. You are and you're not in a city, stretching for one hundred and fifty kilometers, with twelve million inhabitants. Such wealth! Such poverty! You feel that Hispanics have a counter-culture, and they make the society, the music, painting (the murals they've created are beautiful)."

To get to LA, we flew to San Francisco, rented a car, and drove down State Route Number 1, the Pacific Coast Highway, stopping off at Big Sur for nine days, honeymooning at paradise on earth. It was our Garden of Eden for a short while. We had two log cabins perched up a steep winding dirt track, a bit north of Big Sur

Post Office; the car groaned up the incline. The owner threw in another cabin, next door, when he heard we were on our honeymoon. No need for a key, he said. No need to lock things up around here; like Singer's Bessie and Sam on their honeymoon in the Catskills. Just enter—and *mazel tov*. Between each cabin was a hot tub. We were lucky, the owner said, November is a lovely month to come to Big Sur, fine weather, dry, not too cold yet.

We sat in the hot tub every night, staring up at late autumn's spangled ceiling. We slept like never before—in quietness. We saw darkness like never before, a great expanse of black nothingness that stretched out forever, the black on black of all blacknesses, blacker than Goya's black. Yet it made our hearts sing, brought us life not death, a holy happiness free of the profane drudge across the sea. I remember scrawling with a gnarled branch a love heart in the sand, on one of the few accessible beaches around, putting Cupid's arrow through it and Corinna's name beside it. Surf pounded the rocks. Cypress trees clung onto the cliff edge. We watched the sandpipers dart near the water's edge and I thought of *The Sandpiper*, Vincente Minnelli's glossy romance from 1965, with Elizabeth Taylor painting on the beach, and Richard Burton admiring her from afar. I was the shadow of Corinna's smile. We watched the sea otters at Point Lobos, ran together in Andrew Molera State Park, drank more Manhattans, our drug of forgetfulness, this time at sunset, at nearby Nepenthe, on its wooden deck, ringside over the Pacific. The bar and restaurant was built in 1949 on land once owned by Orson Welles and wife Rita Hayworth. Welles dreamt of building his own private idyll there. But it never happened as he imagined.

I was beguiled by Big Sur, stunned by its nature, by its peace, and a beauty never before seen or heard by a lad from Liverpool. I was confused; I was a man of cities, not of nature, of wilderness. How could I fall for all this? Then I remembered how another pacer of city streets, Henry Miller, that patriot of Brooklyn's Fourteenth Ward, had likewise been beguiled by Big Sur. Miller lived here for eighteen years, wrote about it in *Big Sur and the Oranges of Hieronymus Bosch*, published in 1957, the same year Jack Kerouac's *On the Road* appeared. Miller left France at the outbreak of war in 1939, journeying to Greece, but then returned to the US in the early 1940s, hating what had happened to his native land, calling it an "air-conditioned nightmare," hating, too, "that old shithole, New York, where I was born."

In 1944, Miller moved to Big Sur and stayed until 1962. *Big Sur and the Oranges of Hieronymus Bosch* celebrates the work of the fifteenth-century Dutch painter, where oranges and other enticing fruits become the "garden of earthly delights." Such was Big Sur for Miller. "Bosch saw through the phenomenal world,"

Miller said, "rendered it transparent, and thus revealed its pristine aspect." Henry's old log cabin on Partington Ridge, fourteen miles south of Big Sur Post Office, is now the "Henry Miller Memorial Library," aka "The Mothership," open daily to public pilgrimages. I had paid my own respects there, speaking about Henry and the library with Magnus Toren, a Swede who has directed the space since 1993. I'd once seen Henry's old pad in Brooklyn Heights, at 91 Remsen Street, when Brooklyn was cheap; now, I stood beneath the wind-chimes, man in plaid shirt, in front of Henry's rustic gaff.

I'd seen a wonderful old black and white photo of Henry from around 1960, sitting in his Big Sur office-shack, cross-legged, dressed in denim shirt and workman's cap, looking very proletarian. He's surrounded by tatty books on shelves and assorted bits of modern art bric-a-brac. Everything looks beautifully ramshackled. On Henry's work station is a worn Gallimard edition of *Dan Yack*, written by a *vieil ami* from his Paris days, the one-armed war veteran, the Swiss writer-poet Blaise Cendrars. Henry looks very content in his shack. He loved the rugged coastline around there, the vast expanse of sea, the Santa Lucia mountains, Big Sur's unmediated sensuality, an antidote to AC America all around him. "This is the face of the earth," he said, "as the Creator intended it to look."

Kerouac paid homage to Miller, too. He came to Big Sur in 1960 to detox after a drunken crack-up, fleeing the media limelight in the wake of *On the Road*'s ginormous success. He stayed at City Lights bookstore owner Lawrence Ferlinghetti's log cabin at Bixby Canyon (near the famous Bixby Bridge). Kerouac had planned to meet the unofficial Beat Godfather, dine at Miller's friend's home with Ferlinghetti in what would be an historic encounter. "His voice on the phone is just like on his records," Kerouac said in his fictionalized memoir *Big Sur*, "nasal, Brooklyn, good guy voice." But Kerouac stood Miller up, eloped to San Francisco, got bored of being alone in the woods, dry, and yearned for his buddies and booze. He ended up dead drunk at North Beach's Vesuvio Café. Later in the evening, feeling guilty, Kerouac picked up the phone, slurring to Miller about coming down. "Well, I'm sorry I didn't get to meet you, Jack," the polite sixty-something Miller said, "but I'm an old man and at ten o'clock it's time for me to go to bed. You'd never make it here until after midnight now."

Jack didn't stick it out too long in Big Sur's paradise. He missed the city, missed his mates, the camaraderie, people, the action. Maybe he missed diners. At heart he was no Thoreau. Yet he resumed heavy drinking, his Faustian bargain; Jack's physical and mental deterioration never let up until his demise in 1969. It happened to me, too: missing the city, I mean. I loved Big Sur, imagined another Milleresque life living there with Corinna, just the two of us against the world, outside of the world. But by Day Eight I started to get itchy feet and began to relish *the idea of Los Angeles*, that it was somewhere south, three hundred and fifty miles down the road, where a great big pink-gray cloud hovered above it. You could see this cloud looming miles off, making you tingle with apocalyptic anticipation. Forget Hollywood: we were headed toward Mike Davis land, an ecology of fear.

I had loved the peace and tranquility in Big Sur. Corinna and I felt relaxed for once, perhaps for the first time, after the wedding planning, our apartment renovations, our neighbors from hell. Corinna baked an amazing pecan pie; I'll never forget its taste. She'd finished her Ph.D. a couple of weeks earlier, submitted, had her dissertation defense, passed, yet didn't know what she wanted to do with her "career." She didn't pursue its theme. She wanted to get into "food," she'd said, study it, write about it, cook it, though how she wasn't sure. But coming to America was important. Like me, she was relieved to be out of London, out of university life, free of it forever—she hoped—breathing fresh air, free air, looking at that perfect blue sky of lost purity.

Then I really started to miss being around *people*, somewhere outside of the house, in a café, anywhere, amid people but not too close to people. In the wilderness, I'd started to crave *books*, being around them, browsing them, drinking coffee someplace near them, perhaps even reading them. But in public. I'd been in Big Sur for barely over a week. But already I was talking about being back in the city again. Books were second nature, maybe more important to me than any first nature. No matter where I lived, how big or quiet or nice my home might be, I knew I always needed to get out of the front door sometimes, regularly, out into the public realm, into a bookstore. I had to be able to browse as part of everyday life. It was hard for me to live without this, without asphalt, without printed paper, someplace I could walk to, read in.

We lucked out in LA, found a nice short-term rental apartment, a little open-planned studio with a raised bedroom at a mezzanine level and a whole side wall floor-to-ceiling window. We were surrounded by luscious vegetation. Everywhere was squeaky clean. I could walk to the Westwood campus in minutes, passing all the mysterious looking frat houses along Hilgard Avenue. The campus was huge, a city within a city. But once inside the building, where I had a temporary office, it was eerie. Names on doors yet doors firmly closed. Nobody was ever around, not even students. The corridors were deserted, spooky. It felt like the morning after the night of the living dead, like some creepy

George Romero movie where zombies had taken over the world and killed everyone; nobody was left and the zombies had cleared out long ago. There were a lot of brainy people here who wrote about alienation; it was obvious why: It was participant observation. UCLA's corridors were microcosms of LA's streets: empty, lifeless. I knew I could never function in this environment. I felt like I was withering after about an hour. I couldn't write a thing. I had an "irresistible urge to plunge into society," Dostoevsky's Underground Man had said; I felt exactly like that then.

We returned our rental car at LAX and for a couple of weeks were carless in California. Bad idea. Corinna tried riding the bus to Downtown LA, exploring Broadway's Grand Central Market, a food emporium she'd soon love, along with the Farmers Market on West 3rd Street. She discovered bluefish and we'd eat it often, in an apricot marinade, our cheap staple. The problem was that a round-trip from Westwood, by bus, took up practically all daylight hours. It was like journeying to the center of the earth and back. You sat on the bus stop's concrete bench and you waited. You waited and waited for the bus to show, alongside patient Latina women who were used to waiting. Without a car you were condemned to walk. You couldn't walk very far because major roads and wide highways cut you off. One place we'd hang out at almost every evening was the nearby Borders bookstore on

Westwood Boulevard, since gone bust with the rest of the Borders book empire. There were books; we could walk there; and it was open late, till midnight at weekends. Unimaginable in London.

I had come to LA to explore something outside myself. Too introverted, I got depressed. I still do. I wanted to find a different angle to the city, to do something political. Once we got ourselves another rental car we started to explore the city farther afield. If you went with LA's white-light flow, and with its red-light gridlock, you could begin to understand those headlights and brake lights. If you stopped that flow, got inside, really got inside it, walked inside it, saw it stationary, close-up, that flowing glamor lost its speed. Without movement, much of LA was a grotty dump. Anybody would recognize this if they ever saw David Lynch's surreal LA noir, *Mulholland Drive*, from 2001, a "love story in the city of dreams." Those dreams were alluring and intoxicating. If you took a hit, like Lynch's Betty, they drew you in, made you dizzy. The famous HOLLYWOOD sign up on Mount Lee in the Hills made you woozy. But the cold turkey reality behind it all was like a disused parking lot, with a broken-down dumpster splattered with graffiti, piled high with garbage.

Lynch gives us a close-up of exactly such a dumpster in *Mulholland Drive*, behind "Winkie's" diner, where a man has a dream about a phantom lurking there. When he goes to investigate with a friend, a menacing street person, looking like the Wild Man of Borneo, steps out. It's shocking, unexpected; we're not sure if this wild man is real or an hallucination. But the dreamer is so terrified that he collapses with fright. Lynch's camera scans behind Winkie's, homing in on what urbanists used to call SLOAP—Space Left Over After Planning. Not that LA ever had much planning. Not that anywhere these days ever has much planning. SLOAPs are redundant spaces nobody wants to see, wants to remember, wants to deal with. They're useless bits of scrap space in between buildings and spaces that have use, have value, particularly economic value. SLOAPs get brushed under the carpet, are neither public nor private. Frequently, they fill up with vagrants who make these spaces their home. *Mulholland Drive* brings SLOAPs to celluloid. It was an LA I could relate to at foot-level, an LA a lot of people populate. Like those Latina women waiting for the bus.

Many are going to work. They clean offices and hotels and restaurants. They labor for long hours for low pay. And it takes them forever to get on the job. They hardly make a living wage. Often the people they service have received a state or federal subsidy, yet they pay their auxiliary staff very little. The story was familiar across America; it was especially vivid in LA with its vast and dispensable reservoir of Latino workers. If ever you talked about cities with anyone at the bus stop, they'd likely want to talk about a living wage. The problem with cities like LA wasn't unemployment; it was finding work that paid you enough to make ends meet. What was going on in LA was fascinating. Its Latino and Latina immigrant workforce brought with them a militancy and class consciousness that helped pioneer "living wage" struggles. In LA, these struggles were channeled through two unions, one representing the Hotel and Restaurant Employees (HERE)—housekeepers, porters, busboys, dishwashers, and food servers; the other the Service Employees' International Union (SEIU), organizing "Justice for Janitors."

Just as radical academics were busy deconstructing Downtown LA's Bonaventure Hotel as an icon of late capitalist postmodernity, Local 11 of HERE was trying to reconstruct the union there. They'd been fighting for a liveable wage inside luxury hotels where union members scrubbed bathtubs and toilets, made beds, waited tables, and dumped trash for a pittance. They deployed disciplined yet flamboyant street and media tactics. Workers became human billboards, held lobby sit-ins, mass boycotts and flying pickets; they demonstrated raucously in the street, staged "coffee-ins" and "Java for Justice," where union members took over whole dining rooms of hotels, ordering coffee all round, leaving hotel guests and diners bemused.

Much the same could be said about SEIU Local 399, who spearheaded "Justice for Janitors." Property prices and land values soared in LA at the same as real estate taxes have stayed notoriously low, meaning landlords and investors reap colossal booty. Yet, relative to the huge increase in profitable space, more and more work has been extracted from fewer and fewer workers. On a standard shift, the typical janitor swept up 45,000 square feet of office space, a lot more than they once did. That's why union representation citywide has surged, to around seventy percent of cleaning staff. Along the way, Local 399 have embarrassed countless office landlords, wreaking havoc with boisterous demonstrations, occupying office complexes, chanting, screaming, and banging drums, blocking major traffic boulevards, becoming human bollards in astonishing acts of bravery, doing it all in trademark bright-red T-shirts. The business press said activists engaged in "zany, obnoxious, and occasionally illegal techniques that seem born more of the burlesque hall than the union hall."

I found all this tremendously inspiring. I got to talk to a lot of courageous people involved in union organizing and living wage campaigns. I learned plenty about individual meanness and collective generosity, how each got inscribed in city life. I learned how labor animates a city, a city of hope. These struggles created a special kind of city, left their imprint in the urban landscape, ensuring LA's moribund public realm came alive. Mike Davis said Latino struggles created a "magical urbanism." This was what happened when you believed in something beyond cynical realism. Cities aren't just about investment into real estate, into bricks and mortar, into property, about throwing up speculative buildings; they're about people's livelihoods, about how people worked as well as lived. Cities were living labor reclaiming a portion of the surplus they created. The urban landscape needed reshaping according to ordinary people's needs, working people's needs. Architecture was about sociology, should be about the urbanization of labor. Wherever and whenever this happened, if ever it happened, there was something magical to behold.

I lucked out in LA for another reason—at least I thought I lucked out. While there I had an interview for an academic job on the East Coast. I flew over and, somehow, got the position, in Worcester, Massachusetts. It was the nearest place to New York I could find work. So I grabbed at it, went for it. I probably knew in advance the job wouldn't work out. So I'm telling you in advance it didn't work out. But it got me to America, got me a Green Card, and, later, got me to New York. I should have suspected the move was crazy. I remember the evening after my interview, some faculty and grad students took me out to dinner, to one of Worcester's nicest restaurants—there weren't many. The waitress wondered what I was doing here with that weird accent. I told her I was going to move to Worcester. Jesus, she said, everybody I know, me included, would do anything to get the hell out of this dump. Where d'ya come from? she wondered. London, I said. She gave me a look, as if I'd lost my mind or something. *Like, you're quitting London to come live in Worcester, Mass.?* she said. For a split second I shuddered, still shudder, when I think about that look.

I should have known it then. I think I did know it then. But I was in denial, had to be in denial because I wanted so much to get out of London, to embark on a new life, a married life, with a tabula rasa. This would be better, I thought, a better job, with more respect than I got in London, in an interesting, new place, an affordable place, a place of opportunity. I thought we had nothing to lose. Corinna was up for it, too. It seems mad that I accepted, that she accepted, agreed to live in a town she'd never actually been to. When she did come, when we looked for someplace to live, we both knew we could never live in a town like Worcester. Each time she walked down Main Street, near campus, every passing car would give out a wolf whistle. The streets were deserted, menacing; the built fabric decayed, abandoned, like parts of Liverpool in the 1970s. But even there, in Liverpool, there were always people about, group humanity, a mutuality of the oppressed.

Here it was total desolation, individuals out alone, without social infrastructure, seemingly without anything, fending for themselves; and there were guns, something scary again. Jane Jacobs warned about deserted streets becoming dangerous streets. "The sidewalk must have users on it fairly continuously," she said, "both to add to the number of effective eyes on the street and to induce the people in buildings along the street to watch the sidewalks." Worcester had no such thing. It was death without as yet life. An old mill town whose mills closed decades ago; high-tech industry hadn't come; it came nearer Boston. Poor immigrants landed in Worcester when factory jobs were disappearing; the town hemorrhaged its tax base. More able people moved out; more desperate people moved in. Boarded-up buildings and abandoned lots littered the landscape. It scared people away. The campus was a little rich island. All around, hard-up folk tried to hustle, sometimes peddling beat-up old furniture, cheap family heirlooms, out on the sidewalk, in pathetic yard sales. It was a city ecology that made for a particular kind of urban entropy.

In lots of ways, this low density, rustbelt urbanism was more Carver country than any Manhattan. One of his tales, "Why Don't You Dance?", sets the broken-down backdrop of Worcester, MA;

I *felt* Worcester again when I reread this story recently. A young couple, setting up home together, drive through a rundown neighborhood and glimpse objects of somebody's discarded life out on a driveway, up for sale. They stop to see. Nobody's about. Then the guy returns, carrying a supermarket bag full of whiskey and beer. The young woman asks the price of the bed. Fifty dollars, he says; she offers forty. Sure, he says. And so it goes, as he gives a price and she knocks him down each time; each time he agrees. They buy up his bed and desk. He sits back in an armchair, on the sidewalk, offers them a drink. They accept. He puts a record on the gramophone. "This record-player is going, too. Cheap. Make me an offer," he says. He pours more whiskey, opens a beer. "Everything goes," he says. The music rings out. "Why don't you dance?" he asks. "Go ahead, it's my yard. You can dance if you want to." The woman turns to him: "You must be desperate or something." A few weeks later, the woman reflects on the yard sale with her friends. "The guy was about middle-aged," she says. "All his things right there in the yard. No lie. We got real pissed and danced. In the driveway. [...] Look at this record-player, the old guy gave it to us. And all these crappy records. Will you look at this shit?"

We didn't live in Worcester, ended up instead in Boston. I commuted fifty miles along the Mass. Pike. I had to buy a car, a

Dodge Neon, in bright turquoise, first car I ever owned. The guy selling it couldn't believe this when I told him. Jane Jacobs always said there were two kinds of people: foot people and car people. I saw—still see—myself in the former camp. Jacobs also said "urban experts never respect what foot people know and value." I never liked driving a car, was always relieved to park it somewhere, to have my feet touch sidewalk again, someplace solid, uninhabited by technology. To walk was freedom. In a car you were a slave to the rhythm. The mobility Kerouac knew in *On the Road* had come to a jam. I never liked Boston, either: too much "England" in the New. Spalding Gray had it about right, getting out of New England, leaping to freedom in New York.

There weren't many places walkable in Worcester, nowhere you'd really want to walk in. Along Main Street, near campus, there were a couple of little stores just about hanging in there: a hairdresser and a café called JB's, after Judy and Bob, a mom and pop affair that became my saving grace; a place to walk to, sit and write in, to get *off* campus, where my brain worked best. Judy reminded me of my mother, an American reincarnation. She waited on people, good-naturedly, with her daughter Kathy; out back Bob cooked and prepared the food. I felt a class bonding with them, more comfortable in their company than with my faculty peers. Theirs was a struggling small business, getting zilch support from anybody. Even the university discouraged students from venturing there, suggesting they stay on campus, frequent the student café, catered by Starbucks.

JB's was always busy. People came and went throughout the day. A few faculty, workmen passing through, the odd local. Most neighborhood people never had the time or money to come spend on food, to sit around all day in a café. Judy told me each month's earnings barely nudged above overheads. There was nothing else they could do, she said, except up their prices, which she didn't want to do. They were fair as they were, she said. Everything seemed to conspire against JB's. They worked hard, had sufficient customers. People liked coming. Judy and Bob did the right thing, were honest, never ripped people off. And yet, they were squeezed on all sides: by the rent and the lease, by suppliers and the tax man, by the university, that great patron of the "local community," who helped them none.

I ate there most days, same thing: a plain bagel with pastrami, a scrap of salad, a macadamia nut cookie for dessert, which I'd dunk in coffee they made to measure, just how I liked it, a sort of short, strong Americano, before anybody called it Americano. I felt all right there. It was homely, insofar as I could remember what "home" meant. JB's was pretty much my office away from my office. Students knew where to find me, outside my usual hours. Judy and Bob often wondered if I ever did any work, never suspecting I never stopped working while I sat there. I wrote a few books in JB's. There was a romance there; it's hard to equate how, in a town I hated.

That romance came alive again for me, not long ago, came alive almost as a sort of nostalgia, watching the movie *The Fighter*, about a real-life boxer who once floored Sugar Ray Leonard, in a welterweight bout from 1978. Sugar Ray won the fight but he did go down. For years it became a legendary event for Lowell; their native son, Dicky Eklund, "the Pride of Lowell," downing Sugar Ray. Sugar Ray always maintained he slipped, or was pushed, wasn't decked by any punch. Footage is fuzzy; both parties have a share of the truth. So the battle got enshrined in Lowell's popular history, along with *On The Road*, written by that other Lowell native, who penned a more beautiful book about Lowell, the haunting *Dr. Sax*.

Outside the ring, Dicky Eklund's life was forever on the ropes. He was a crackhead throughout the 1980s and 1990s, got involved in petty larceny, served time in the state pen; *The Fighter*, starring Christian Bale as Dicky, retells his colorful tale, bedding itself down in another deindustrialized mill town, forty-five miles northeast of Worcester. Each time I watch its opening sequence, with Dicky and his younger half-brother, champion boxer Micky Ward (played by Mark Wahlberg), parading through Lowell's backstreets, with an HBO camera in tow, and The Heavy's "How You Like Me Now?" blaring out, mixed memories of Worcester come flooding back.

Like two working-class Pied Pipers, Dicky and Micky pass by the barbershop and the pawnbroker's, corner stores and boarded-up stores, encountering local hoodlums and ordinary stiffs, druggies and cops on the beat, good guys and wise guys, all cameoing as a sub-stratum of Carveresque America. HBO did actually make that documentary, about Eklund's crack addiction, a substance abuse that back then, mid-1990s, was ravaging urban America. *High on Crack Street: Lost Lives in Lowell*, a harrowing hour-long portrayal of how crack disintegrates people's lives, follows Dicky, a pregnant prostitute, Brenda, and her abusive boyfriend/pimp Boo-Boo, around their destructive and self-destructive everyday life; much the same drama could have easily unfolded further southwest, down Interstates 495 and 290, in Worcester.

Late one afternoon, when Judy was sweeping up, preparing to close for the day, I stayed late and we had a chat. These past few weeks, she said, she'd been feeling exhausted. She wasn't sure what was wrong with her, not having the same energy as before. Long days on her feet, little respite during the day, no vacation; evenings she just flakes out in front of the TV. She can't do anything anymore. She doesn't know how long she can keep this going, keep the business afloat. She loves what she's doing here, but it's taking its toll. I told her she's working too hard; back off a bit, take a few days off. Bob and Kathy can manage for a while.

Several weeks on, Judy hadn't been around for a few days. I asked Kathy what had happened to her, hoping she'd taken time away. But Kathy said she'd been feeling bad. She was at home today, spent the morning in bed, unable to get up. She might want to call the doctor, I said. Then a week or so on, Judy reappeared at JB's. She's out back, Kathy said, if you want to go and see her. It was the first time I'd been backstage at JB's and remember the distressing sight of Judy, sitting there, in rapid decline, just like my old ma years before: her yellowing complexion, a bloated, sick look on her face, a knowing resignation in those eyes. I knew then, as maybe she did, she'd not long left. Her cancer had advanced. It was very distressing. A couple of weeks later, Judy was dead.

Afterward, Kathy took over JB's. Judy's death affected Bob. He started to behave weirdly. One day he didn't show up, never ever came back, had run off with a much younger woman. Kathy, left by herself, was miffed about her dad. She hired a young girl to help out. But it was the beginning of the end. Like a lot of small businesses, they'd been staring down the abyss; now, the abyss stared back. Not long after I'd quit Worcester, I heard JB's had closed for good. I shed a tear when I found out. I'd had some good memories from JB's, remembering I wrote my first "hit" piece there, my review of Marshall's *Adventures in Marxism*.

I'd written this piece for my own amusement, as is often the case. This time, though, I decided to look up *The Nation*'s literary editor, a guy called Art Winslow, and sent him a copy via e-mail. I thought it might fit *The Nation*, had nothing to lose. Might as well. Though, as ever, I believed I'd dispatched it into a black hole, to be swallowed up by another editor's event horizon, never to be seen or heard of again, lost forever. It had happened many times in the UK. And yet, a few days on, one dull morning, sitting at my desk in Worcester, feeling lonely, infused with all the dullness of a workaday university office, I turned my old Mac on and discovered a two-line e-mail from Art Winslow. "Got your Berman piece. Give me a call at 212–...." I thought I was seeing things, dreaming or something.

Surely this guy wouldn't ask me to call to say he wasn't interested? That would've been unprecedented, far too decent. As it happened, Art was laid-back about it, actually kind. He liked the piece, thought he could use it. He asked me what my relationship with Berman was. Sure, I said, I knew Berman a bit, not well, was getting to know him better, since I've just moved to the US. I knew and admired his work, had read him for ages. Okay, Art said, I'm gonna take it, put it in next week's issue. I'll get the galleys faxed over to you, probably tomorrow morning, if you give me a number. See you… And that was that. He didn't know me, had no idea who I was. Yet, by some miracle of meritocracy, he'd take it anyhow.

"A Dialectical Humanism" appeared the following week. An unfortunate title, not my own. I'd spent years trying to rid myself of crippling academic speak and coming to the US helped, hearing ordinary idiom spoken in cafés like JB's. Now, suddenly, a non-academic weekly goes all academic on me! I'd called my review "A Marxist Urban Romance." Marshall's adventures in Marxism had, after all, been an urban romance. Without realizing it, it was maybe the first time I'd written about love. Marshall wasn't bothered with flows of capital or "scientific" political-economy. His vision of Marxism and the city was a love affair that fleshed out subjectivity, expressed happiness and joy; and he usually translated this experience through his own dialectical self. He was always there, in the dialogue, in the narrative flow, converting Empson's seven types of ambiguity into the poetry of his own tormented self.

The personal was political for Marshall, although something more than that clichéd, flat-tire turn of phrase, something more nuanced. The personal *should be* political, because, he said, politics should be more personal, more felt. In his adventures in Marxism, the self got "caught up in the mix." "Caught Up in the Mix" was Marshall's intro to *Adventures in Marxism*, a collection of essays previously published in *Dissent*, *The Nation*, *New Left Review*, *The New York Times Book Review*, etc. In this particular case you could judge a book by its cover: a dancing, zoot-suited Karl Marx, who, despite his advancing years and big gray mane, still knew a few slick moves, grooving to Sixties rock and roll, a street-fighting man demanding the world and wanting it *now*; but that gleaming blue zoot suit suggested a jazzier Marx (and Marshall), a Fifties re-tread, mellow and free, improvised and syncopating to bebop. Marshall had his millennial sage straddle both decades, affirming a Marxism and a self that was melodic and ironic, and somehow loud, rough, and sexual, too.

Before *Adventures in Marxism*'s release, I'd heard Marshall read "Caught Up in the Mix" aloud, as he customarily did with his work, at the now-defunct Brecht Forum, located in a grungy loft space on West 27th Street. Corinna and I made a special journey down from Boston, just to see Marshall, staying overnight in a little hotel we knew on Riverside Drive, a couple of blocks west of Zabar's. I think Marshall was thrilled and touched to see us attend. The crowd that night was sparse, on the older side—the "Used Left," Marshall might have called it; he joked about his own generation, in its heyday once the "New Left." Marshall read out with enormous poignancy lines about his father who'd worked himself to death—wasn't even forty-eight when he died—and how business partner, Dave, ran off with the earnings of their small garment firm, Betmar Tag & Label Company, near Times Square. Each time Marshall read from Marx's *Economic and Philosophic Manuscripts*, as a direct quotation, he'd raise his hand and put on a serious drawl so the audience knew it was Karl rather than Marshall talking.

"Caught Up in the Mix" was a *Bildungsroman* of a precocious scholar discovering the early manuscripts of a similarly precocious scholar, a "Karl Marx before he became Karl Marx." Here was a text, Marshall said, that could help us figure out how we're all thrown together in the mix, in the capitalist mix, and how we could fight for the power to remix, perhaps doing some mixing ourselves. "I've got to have this book!"—*The Economic and Philosophic Manuscripts*, he meant—young Berman demanded of the calm "white-haired clerk" at the Four Continents radical bookstore, the official distributor for Soviet publications near Union Square, now long gone of course. "Right there," Marshall said, "my adventure began." Almost before he started reading young Marx's *Manuscripts*, Marshall began proclaiming to everyone: "It'll show you how our whole life's wrong, but it'll make you happy, too."

Later that year, in the fall, I heard Marshall read this same piece out again, in Cambridge, at WordsWorth Books in Harvard Square (now also no more), after *Adventures in Marxism* had gone public. By then I was in the throes of my teaching so decided to corral a bunch of grad students to tag along. I told them this guy Berman was the real thing, and they should come and see. Arrive early, I said, because, given it was Harvard, Marshall's alma mater—where he'd written a doctoral thesis on Rousseau and Montesquieu—there'd be a big crowd. Seating would be limited.

That same week my review of *Adventures in Marxism* featured in *The Nation*; even better, Marshall loved it, was telling everybody about it! He liked how I'd managed to review his book and get some of my own material into it, too, making it original, he said, a learned essay rather than standard review. I was making his adventure in Marxism my adventure in Marxism, he said, with typical generosity. I was psyched about this Cambridge event, felt I'd begun to make my mark, in public, as a writer. It might have been something of an ambition in those days. But showing up at WordsWorth I was stunned to find nobody there, apart from my crew, the moderator, and Marshall himself. After a while, a couple more stragglers showed up, totaling about ten people in all. Without me, and my little posse of fellow-travelers, it would have been almost an empty house. How could this be so? I was naïve back then, hadn't recognized how Harvard was an institution full of professional and wannabe-professional academics; their careers were too important to bother to show up for a humanistic poetry reading.

I was catching on how Marshall was an intellectual outcast, a scholar who loved ideas for the love of those ideas. All he ever wanted was to share this love with the world. But that wasn't what made academia tick. Maybe it never did. There was nothing in it for those Ivy League pros. Marshall, on the other hand, didn't have an instrumentalist bone in his body. Afterward, he told me he wasn't surprised by the lack of turnout at WordsWorth. He said he was the Fritz Lang of urban studies, a cult, arthouse draw, never a man for the straight-laced. He was a chip off the old block of where academia was headed, and he knew it, was old enough to get beyond it. His personality, his style of criticism, his jargon-free rap, his "jaytalking," as he called his conversational style—all seemed far off the conventional university radar. It was a space I wanted to occupy.

I had another piece in *The Nation* soon after, about a kindred soul of Marshall's, a romantic urbanist from an earlier generation: Walter Benjamin. For years the German essayist and critic sat under the "painted sky of summer"—the massive ceiling mural of Paris's Bibliothèque Nationale—scribbling his "dialectical fairy-tale," *The Arcades Project*, freshly translated into English. I pitched the idea of a review to Art Winslow who'd responded positively. It was a great brick of a book that wasn't really any recognizable book at all. More a gigantic maze of citations and ideas, gossip and rumination, lists and quips, elliptical evocations, commentaries on commentaries. Benjamin once said he wanted to produce a work consisting entirely of quotations; here he'd pretty much achieved it. Little of anything was developed; rarely was there continuity between themes and thoughts; and the narrative—if you could call it a narrative—flits about at Benjamin's whim. It was great.

Benjamin said *The Arcades Project* was "the theater of all my struggles and all my ideas." Thirteen years in the making, Benjamin aimed big, sought to chronicle the whole history of the nineteenth century, over which Paris, he said, presided. He'd been beguiled by the City of Light ever since a two-week trip in 1913—"the most beautiful experience"—made during his Berlin student days. That year was significant in another respect: Benjamin attended the packed lectures given by the brilliant *fin-de-siècle* modernist Georg Simmel, whose *The Philosophy of Money* and *The Metropolis and Mental Life* left an indelible impression on the rookie Benjamin, underwriting how he'd think about big cities. Like his former teacher, Benjamin knew how the metropolis "intensified emotional life," presented "continuous shifts of external and internal stimuli." It was a big city thing: the metropolis's sheer tempo, its innumerable interactions and encounters, its dissonance and unexpected upheavals, contrasted with the slower and smoother rhythm of the small town. For good reason did Benjamin look upon Paris as "a landscape built of sheer life."

In such a setting, modern men and women bloomed. Benjamin yearned to bloom, too, as he worked through the metropolis's dialectical basis. On the one hand, he knew cities were the seats of giant economies, of great big divisions of labor and exchange; money was the common measure of value, the equivalent of all human worth. Every quality got reduced to quantity, everybody thrown into objective relationships and obligatory associations. Alienation ensued. The city became Célinesque, a death on credit.

And yet, on the other hand, this was paradoxically the root of immense developmental tendencies as well, offering tremendous scope for individual and collective freedom. Now metropolitan life opened up human potentiality, enlarged your frame of reference. People could breathe, lose their fixed identities, liberate themselves from small-town binds. Thus the modern metropolis—nineteenth-century Paris, twentieth-century New York—was, is, a "seat of cosmopolitanism." Now Benjamin's city suddenly became Whitmanesque, a lighthearted open road. So

Benjamin, the Marxist critic, condemned the metropolis with its ruthless money economy, recoiled in horror from its crass material trappings and its oppressions, excesses, and inequalities. Meanwhile, he reveled in the city's exuberance as a seat of cosmopolitanism, drenched himself in its heady atmosphere, danced to its luminous flow.

Benjamin was perhaps our greatest twentieth-century urban Marxist and hence one of the most troubled Marxist thinkers, a man after Marshall's own heart, another angel in the city. People across America, especially middle-class white people, go on retreating into their suburban havens and gated communities; shopping malls no longer bolster street life but happily undermine it, purposely disengage from any sidewalk convulsion; yet Benjamin romantically upheld the central city street. His city was full of pedestrians, sexiness, and bustling streets. In these streets, outside became inside, and plain-old walkers became dandies and *flâneurs* who "blush before the eyes of no one." In The *Arcades Project*, Benjamin sang a paean to an expansive and inclusive urban public space, one that internalized the whole world.

When, in 1940, he trekked across the Pyrenean foothills, gripping the black briefcase stuffed with his *Arcades* manuscript, in Benjamin's pocket was a US entry visa. He'd stagger along the rolling mountain trail near the Spanish border, amid the vine stalks of Banyuls, for ten minutes, stop, rest a minute, then proceed at the same pace, edging toward freedom, dragging the black monster with the sun beating down. Lisa Fittko, Benjamin's guide, together with their companions fleeing the Nazis, took turns carrying the bag, which rarely left Benjamin's gaze. It was more valuable to him than anything else, Fittko said, even his own life. At Portbou, hours later, we find Benjamin true to his word. A bureaucratic quirk prevented anybody exiting France that day. Exhausted, unable to take any more, on the evening of September 25, with the Gestapo moving in, Benjamin swallowed his entire morphine supply, all fifty tablets. He was dead by morning.

He'd had New York firmly in his sights. Two years earlier he wrote to "Teddie" Adorno, from Bertolt Brecht's Danish retreat, describing how he'd been studying the details of Manhattan's streets on a map stuck to Brecht's son's bedroom wall. "I walk up and down," Benjamin told his comrade in New York, "the long street on the Hudson where your house is." He never did take that stroll up Riverside Drive. He would have doubtless felt at home amid the Jewish émigré culture of the Upper West Side, might have taught at the New School, chatted with I. B. Singer feeding his pigeons. Benjamin would have loved Upper Broadway, with its constant ebb and flow of people and intricate ballet. But he would have been appalled by New York's crackdown on the homeless and intolerance toward street vendors and shambling habitués of its sidewalks.

One reason I loved Walter Benjamin and wanted to write about his long-lost manuscript was that he was one of the twentieth-century's most tragic bunglers, a nearly man: someone who nearly received critical acclamation, who nearly secured that steady university job and book contract, who nearly made it to daylight. I sort of related to that side of him. Maybe Marshall did, too. Benjamin was also one of the century's biggest brains and most original thinkers, somebody still ahead of his time. He marveled at Paris, made loyal friends with books and with characters in books, haunted library stacks as much as streets, yearned for literary recognition but never got it.

My review made the front page of *The Nation*. It had been my greatest literary thrill to date, perhaps still is. I was in New York again, witnessing it hot off the press, the evening it came out, there on another trip with Corinna. We'd found a moderate-priced B&B on the Upper West Side, on West 69th Street, a little walk-up one-bedroomed pad. We weren't sure how things were going to pan out in such a small space. It turned out the occupant rented out her own bed to guests, making an extra bit of cash on the side, flouting co-op rules but finding a way to make the monthly maintenance charge. She'd take the living room sofa while we took her bedroom. She served us stale croissants for breakfast and lukewarm coffee and not much else. She owned the place outright, paid off the mortgage long ago, had retired from whatever she'd done in her life; now, on a fixed income, it was a struggle to pay the monthly maintenance, which always rose. I'd soon discover it was a familiar trait. The building had a good year, residents were told, finances were healthy, all major repair works done; and yet, and yet…the management company was shoving up the maintenance charge anyway, just in case, just to be on the safe side, for the future, you know. It was a racket. And a lot of elderly New Yorkers suffered through that racket.

It was a brutally cold January. I remember walking down Broadway late Saturday evening, very late. The breeze tore into any bare flesh. I wore ski gloves and my rabbit-skin cap, flaps turned down, covering my ears. The wind chill, whistling between buildings, blowing off the Hudson, made everything seem even more freezing than New England. I had raced up forty blocks to the international newsagent between 112th and 113th Streets, with its vast array of global press, around the corner from Labyrinth bookstore, near Seinfeld's diner, and found that week's *Nation*. I was delirious, drunk with pride, and floated down a deserted sidewalk, down another forty blocks, fighting off frostbite, eager to show Corinna who was sound asleep by the time I made it back alive.

The Nation became an important outlet for me not because of its relatively large readership; it was more a personal thing. I'd found in its pages my writer's voice, the way I wanted to write, the mode of expression I wanted to advance—for myself, not for anybody else. It was always strange for me, anyhow, this notion that somebody might want to read what I'd written. Corinna and I thought that happiness might not be the meaning of life. We might find happy moments, perhaps, if we got lucky, had already found a few. We *were* lucky there. But the idea that happiness would define our life together wasn't realistic. We both agreed. We both felt that *self-expression* was where it was at; a privilege, we knew, but a necessity nonetheless.

My need to express myself, to communicate and commune on the page, with a text, with words, with ideas, with books and writers I loved, was even more vital to me than any job, certainly any academic job. I saw that in Walter Benjamin, understood his deep need, the need to express himself, come what may. What he wrote was often so idiosyncratic I'm not sure he ever thought anybody would read it. It was never designed to be popularly read, to be read by anybody. His writings never really fitted in anywhere, were beyond categorization. I felt a modest ontological bonding with him. In fact, the more I discovered my writer's voice, and the intellectual path I wanted to travel along, the more it seemed to diverge from what I did in a university. Paths split at a major intersection; I'd reached that intersection. Me and Corinna both agreed: we *needed* New York now, needed to be there. We were ready to be there. How amazing would that be?

Hitherto, Corinna had passed her time, almost all her day, in the Boston Public Library along Boylston Street, beavering away beneath its little emerald desk lanterns. She was reading up on every aspect of food, from farm to fork, gate to plate—cooking and nutrition, policy and trade, retailing and advertising—the whole gamut of culinary experience, in the US, across the world. She'd been hanging out with New England's organic farmers, too, and getting involved in local Community Supported Agriculture (CSA), redoubling her desire to express herself through food, to venture where her dear mother never dared venture. She had also discovered the Union Square farmers' market, got to know its upstate farmers, who piled down into Manhattan, selling not only their wonderful produce but also making Union Square one of New York's most dynamic and interesting public spaces, especially on Saturdays, fending off the not so interesting retail chains that surround it on all sides. The city's "natural" beauty was being redefined by farmers from the countryside.

We had the idea of finding a little pied-à-terre in Manhattan, on the Upper West Side. Come every weekend, we thought, get ensconced in the city, see where that led. We wanted to test out Benjamin's thesis: that New York was "a landscape built on sheer life," a place and a culture where we could self-express and self-develop, do it alongside others with similar yearnings, making ourselves a home while feeling at home. We looked at many dark and dismal studios, between 72nd and 96th Streets, Riverside Drive and Central Park West, a lot facing stark brick walls splattered in bird shit, illuminated by natural light barely a minute each day, when the sun peeked between neighboring buildings. Others were so tiny it was hard to take two paces before you'd encounter one of its four walls, unable to swing a proverbial cat.

Then we found an unusual one, which nobody seemed to want, low maintenance, on the market a while, a ground floor on 93rd Street, near Columbus Avenue. It looked like it may have once been a superintendent's office, or his tool closet, because you'd enter its front door *before* you entered the building itself. When the building's front door got locked up, we were still on the outside, the wrong side of the entry hall. Inside its walls, though, the kitchen had been redone, completely modernized, amenable to micro-living, surprisingly well equipped. We saw how we could build French windows to convert what was essentially one room into two rooms, then line the walls with bookshelves, get a nice sofa bed, and create our own little nest, which was really more a fish bowl, sunken below sidewalk level. Light flooded in; yet we were totally exposed to the street, two little tadpoles swimming merrily around a vast ocean. We loved it, decided to buy it, to see if the co-op board would have us. Then we recruited Marshall to pen us a recommendation, spellbind them with a few of his magical words.

We recognized pretty quickly what we could do to make such a little space fit our needs, fit our personalities, pledging that it could become something more than a weekend crash pad. We could come and live here all the time, permanently. Corinna remembered a Carole King lyric: "I always wanted a real home with flowers on the window sill / But if you want to live in New York City, honey, you know I will." We could make it work, with a bit of imagination—romantic imagination. In the meantime, until something else showed up, I'd commute to Worcester, for my anti-romance, maybe find a room up there a few days each week, cram my teaching in, gradually decouple from the bad scene, its bad karma. I'd already decided I wasn't giving them tenure.

Marshall was enthusiastic about our coming. Terrif, he said. New York needs people like you, newcomers who care about it, who have the emotional resources to care, who open themselves up to the city, embrace it, who want to live here rather than grudgingly come for work here. He said as much in his co-op board letter. I'm not sure the board really understood what he meant. I remember Marshall saying, shortly afterward, something like: you have to love New York for its faults, you have to learn how to live with its faults, embrace them, embrace everything, warts and all. You have to look the negative in the face and live with it. Marshall knew I knew this was Hegel's maxim, the speculative German philosopher who taught Marx plenty. In 1807, Hegel said: "Spirit is a power only by looking the negative in the face and living with it. Living with it is the magic power that converts the negative into being."

This was classic Marshall, his energy of thought. It was how he could be a *positive* critic, a man whose life and thought derived its strength from the depressive position, from the critic as artist. "The life of the spirit isn't the life that shrinks from death and keeps itself untouched by devastation," said Hegel, "but rather the life that endures it and maintains itself in it. It wins its truth only when, in utter dismemberment, it finds itself." This is maybe why Marshall could write memorable lines like: "Even as New York fell apart, it rose." I wonder now, hearing Marshall's voice in my head, whether he was really warning me somehow, telling me something I should heed, should have heeded, thought I was able to heed: looking the negative in the face and living with it, not walking away from it.

So we came in the summer, without fanfare. Just a U-Haul trailer. Thirty years in the making, the culmination of a dream, a little boy once atop the Empire State Building now niched up, as a man, sixty blocks uptown. I was here. We were here. Or was it there, because it took me a while to believe it was true, that I actually was *here*, that I hadn't just fallen down a big rabbit hole and that, soon, I'd have to wake up to the recognition that it never really happened. It was a terrifying nightmare, haunting me by day: that somebody would take this New York life away from me.

That first summer Corinna and I had never been in such close proximity before, neither of us having an office to go to. We had to adjust. We had one desk, and one computer, next to the window, or rather under the window, in full view of passersby. We didn't want to kill the daylight with blinds. We weren't precious about privacy. I liked writing about public space with public space entering my living (and bed) room. Neighborhood kids used to linger outside, intrigued, foreheads pressed against the bars, fascinated by what was going on inside, mesmerized by the Plaza Hotel we had on the window ledge—the little tin box containing our tea stock, modeled on the Central Park South hotel that Scott Fitzgerald immortalized.

When Walter Benjamin spoke about the arcades' inside becoming outside, and the outside becoming inside, blurring any definitive public-private separation, between architecture and the street, we knew what he was talking about: it was our everyday—and every night—lived reality. We inhabited a sort of arcade, a glass edifice in which we tried to make the charming fruitful; the street was our living room; the public space outside, was ours. Our backyard was Central Park. We had a shift routine over computer use. In the mornings and early afternoon, between nine and one, I had it, would tap away at my stuff, from handwritten notes, and Corinna disappeared, sometimes to the Public Library on Fifth Avenue and 42nd Street. But I had to be out, absolutely had to—house rules—by one p.m., so she could work at home for the rest of the day. She needed the computer more than I did. She was doing well, freelancing here and there, writing reports for British NGOs, self-educating, earning a bit of money.

In the afternoon, I'd wander around Manhattan—principally, I'd wander. I remember reading a French novel called *All The King's Horses*, by Michèle Bernstein, from 1960, her thinly disguised account of living with husband Guy Debord, another urbanist hero of mine, an experimental filmmaker, sometime militant, and poet. Bernstein's book gave an artful glimpse of Debord's—or "Gilles," as he's called in the text—peripatetic habits, *flâning* around Paris. Gilles, we hear, is both too young and too old for the times. "What do you work as?" somebody asks him. "How do you occupy your time?" "With reification," Gilles answers. "That's very serious work, I imagine, with lots of thick books and lots of papers on a grand table," the interlocutor quips. "No," says Gilles, "I wander, principally I wander."

So there it was: principally, in the afternoons, until early evening, no matter the weather or my mood, each day, I'd wander. I'd find somewhere to pen a few words, to read a few lines, and then move on to the next place, sniffing out a bookstore somewhere in between, wandering around, always on the lookout for novel experiences and interesting sights, for sheer life.

One lunchtime staging post was Columbus Bakery, with its yellow, sliced bread signage out front, along Columbus Avenue near 83rd Street, now part of New York's minor history, likely missed by few although memorable to me. One time I saw the cultural critic and Columbia University scholar, Edward Said, there, looking gaunt with a beard, not long left to live, dying of leukemia, wearing a smart brown tweed suit. Another time, actor-comedian Robin Williams exited as I entered, sporting a baseball cap, feeding on a sandwich to go, muttering to himself, maybe rehearsing lines for his latest film. Had he known he would commit suicide years later? I didn't like Columbus Bakery much.

Not an ideal writer's café. But it was there, convenient, and its salads, while overpriced, were edible—unlike other Upper West Side cafés.

Lining up was always slow going, exasperating when hungry. Often the place was too crowded; tables squeezed together, a little too close for a writer's comfort, for obtaining that personal space you needed, where your mind could wander within your text. In an ideal writer's café, there had to be sufficient ambient noise around, to feel like the surrounding area is full, yet not too full, nor too empty, either. Emptiness meant being noticed, sitting there visible, exposed, hence vulnerable. You had to be *incognito*, a person in the crowd, of the crowd but not *with* the crowd. It was highly subjective, this balance between fullness and emptiness, between a café that had enough space to let your mind and pen free up, offsetting your aloneness.

I would sit and eat and read through the printout of my morning's activity, annotating, revising and revisiting some more. No such thing as good writing, somebody once told me, only good rewriting. I'd slash words, lose them, hack them to bits so that it sounded right. Isaac Babel said "no iron can stab the heart with such force as a period put just at the right place." Carver liked to quote that one. He wanted to pin it up somewhere, as a tradesman's reminder, "on a three-by-five." "I go over each sentence time and time again," Babel said. "I start by cutting out all the words I can do without. Words are very sly. The rubbishy ones go into hiding." And yet no voice can penetrate your own head space. If somebody nearby, or even faraway, talked too loudly, or at a frequency you picked up on, couldn't switch off, it was the end. Time to leave, move on. Wandering helped.

One of my favorite books about a writer's wandering relationship with the city is Peter Handke's *The Afternoon of a Writer*. When Handke's nameless writer wandered, "it seemed to him that he wasn't going away from his work but that it was accompanying him; that, now far from his desk, he was still at work." Handke's writer muses how strange it is "that someone in his profession always felt most at home out of doors." Still, "even when walking about alone," he said, "he knew that a few people were concerned, each in their own way, with the same questions, and were pursuing the same aims, as himself; he had not wanted to meet these doubles, he was content to share the ground under their feet, the wind, the weather, daybreak and nightfall with them." That was why my wanderings were *New York wanderings*.

Another lunchtime destination, wandering farther westward, was Edgar's Café, on West 84th Street, tucked away between West End Avenue and Broadway, off the beaten track. That section of West 84th Street is Edgar Allan Poe Street, named after one of America's most famous poets and scribe of short macabre tales. The moustached man himself adorns the café's wall, a canvas of him looking typically glum, full of pathos. Edgar's Café pays homage to the writer who penned perhaps the nation's best-known poem, "The Raven," on this very site, formerly the Brennen Farmhouse, where Poe lived between March 1844 and August 1845.

Last time I was there, revisiting Edgar's, not so long ago, a gray bust of the said black bird gently rapped at the building's chamber door, with a plaque commemorating poor Poe beside it, reminding us that the destitute and tuberculosed poet, dead at forty, wandered these parts, cane in hand, in frockcoat and cravat, all black. "Get thee back into the tempest and the Night's Plutonian shore!" "Leave my loneliness unbroken!—Take thy beak from out of my heart, and take thy form from off my door!" Alas, the café itself was gone, another victim, I'd surmised, of New York's real estate market; or was it the café was just too out of the way, fittingly furtive in its Poe-like marginality, a commercial space on a non-commercial block? Few people knew of its existence. Unlike Columbus Bakery, despite its more refined menu and dignified ambiance—pastel-colored walls, sepia lighting—Edgar's was rarely busy. Its emptiness often made too much noise. I liked places a little more peopled, where my "deep crime," as

Poe said, was "I refused to be alone," that I yearned to be "a man of the crowd." Mercifully, Edgar's Café hadn't closed its doors: it had merely gotten displaced, purloined to another Upper West Side location, now along Amsterdam Avenue, between 91st and 92nd Streets, alive and kicking, still rap-tapping at the door, still serving my preferred avocado salad.

Poe had an admirer across the ocean, another urban talker and scribbler of verse, a tireless stalker of cities, Charles Baudelaire, one of Walter Benjamin's heroes. Baudelaire had written appreciatively about the American poet in 1852, in the *Revue de Paris*. In the mid-1850s, he'd translated Poe's "Raven," along with *Tales of Mystery and Imagination*, finding Gallic fraternity, shared ideas about life and art, and about the psychology of cities. Both men saw city life as their great muse. The crowd was their domain. They wanted to dwell in its throng, in the continuous tides of population—in the bustle of modern urbanity, in what Baudelaire called "the fleeting and the infinite."

Our cities are rich in poetic and wonderful subjects; the marvelous envelops us everywhere, Baudelaire said, "but we fail to see it." In Poe's tale "The Man of the Crowd," from 1840, its narrator talks about how "the tumultuous sea of human heads filled me with a delicious novelty of emotion." "I gave up, at length," he said, "all care of things and became absorbed in contemplation of the scene without." "The wild effects of the light enchanted me," he went on, "to an examination of individual faces; and although the rapidity with which the world of light flitted before the window, prevented me from casting more than a glance upon each visage, still it seemed that, in my then peculiar mental state, I could read, even in that brief interval of a glance, the history of long years."

I'd learned so much reading Marshall, reading him reading Baudelaire, Poe, and Benjamin, that his spirit tracked my peregrinations around New York almost with every step. Perhaps I was really stalking him, following Marshall's bearded phantom, just as Poe's narrator, hurriedly putting on an overcoat and seizing his hat and cane, followed the phantom man of the crowd. I have a photograph of Marshall which I kept secret until recently. The image is intrusive, taken on the sly, done without Marshall's consent. I hardly knew him then, when it was taken, one chilly spring afternoon, over twenty years ago. He's donned in CCNY jacket, in his element, out in the public realm, on the street, his street, Upper Broadway, outside the Metro Diner, about to enter.

His image seems evermore poignant, as I look at it again, because that's where Marshall died. I hummed and harred about showing the picture to anybody, even about talking about it. But in the end thought I would, thought Marshall wouldn't mind, wouldn't mind because he always said images and ideas should be shared, should be part of a common culture. What strikes looking at the photo is, relative to the scale of everything, relative to the other people on the street, to the buildings, to the whole cityscape, how small Marshall looks. He's an anonymous man in the crowd, looking ragged and moth-eaten, like a cross between an Old Testament prophet and a homeless vagrant, a "homeless genius," as someone once called him, an anti-hero from the pages of Poe and Baudelaire, or from Dostoevsky and Gogol, an Akaky Akakievich searching for his stolen overcoat, an underground man battling the structures of power that dominate and tower over him.

A friend of mine, not an academic, took this photo, when I was inside the Metro Diner, waiting for Marshall to arrive. It was during my pre-Corinna days. I'd come to New York with an old school chum. I've since lost contact with him, not seen or heard of him for years. We entered later phases of our lives. But I kept his photograph. My friend had wanted to get Marshall on camera, on the street. A month prior, at the Oxford conference I'd co-organized, hearing Marshall talk about rap music and social justice in America, my friend was blown away. Marshall read from James Joyce's *Ulysses*, from the "Nestor" episode, and it really touched my friend. In that episode, the young schoolteacher, Stephen Dedalus, encounters Mr. Deasy, the old reactionary headmaster. "All human history," says Mr. Deasy, "moves towards one great goal, the manifestation of God." Stephen is unimpressed. "History," he says, "is a nightmare from which I am trying to awake." And, jerking his thumb toward the window, where school kids play hockey outside, adds: "That is God. Hooray! Ay! Whrrwhee!" "What?" wonders Mr. Deasy. "A shout in the street," answers Stephen, shrugging his shoulders.

The pages of *All That Is Solid* devoted to "Modernism in the Streets" are particularly inspiring, some of the best Marshall ever wrote. And he was proud to have written them: "People have especially enjoyed my take on Baudelaire," he said, "on the connections between metropolitan life and inner life." "I've had many happy hours 'doing' Baudelaire, bringing out his romance of a city of crowds, vibrating with mutual fantasy and desire." "Baudelaire imagines a new form of writing that is also a new form of urban development," Marshall said, "and also a new form of democratic citizenship, and also a new way of being alive."

I've often wondered whether this is Baudelaire talking, or Marshall? I'm rooting for Marshall: he makes Baudelaire better, more hopeful, less exclusively French, more universal, more eternal: so long as we have cities, Marshall's Baudelaire will always lurk around some dark corner. As ever, it's an interpretation that comes with a dialectical twist, a dialectical sting. "We can hope, as Baudelaire sometimes hoped, for a future in which joy and beauty, like the city lights, will be shared by all," Marshall said. "But our hope is bound to be suffused by the self-ironic sadness that permeates Baudelaire's city air."

When T. S. Eliot said, "Baudelaire created a mode of release and expression for other men," I felt the same about Marshall: that reading him created a mode of release and expression for me. I hung out a lot with Marshall after I moved to New York. He was the person in town I got to know best, saw him frequently, began to call him a friend. I like to think he thought the same about me. He always made an effort to see me, put himself out. He tried to incorporate me into his daily life over that first summer, which revolved around child-minding, looking after son Danny, a little boy back then. We'd go and sit in the park, often on a bench at one of Central Park's numerous playgrounds. Danny would run around and play with other kids, jump in the sandbox, slide down the slides; Marshall and I would keep an eye out and talk. He'd wear his tie-dye t-shirt, shorts, and sandals, looking like the Sixties hippie he was.

I wanted to ask him everything. But you needed to go easy, you had to slow things down with Marshall, take your time. Danny would run back and forth. Our conversations hobbled along, according to Danny's ebbing and flowing, his coming and going. "Whenever the children ran," Grace Paley once said, "their mothers stopped to talk." It was a bit like that with me and Marshall; only he was a rare dad. "Just when I most needed important conversation," said Paley, in that same short story, "Faith in a Tree," set in a New York playground, "a sniff of the man-made world, at least one brainy companion who could translate my friendly language into his tongue…I was forced to lounge in our neighborhood park, surrounded by children." It was a lone mother's frustration, Paley being ironic; but sitting there, you got a sense of what she meant. Marshall knew what she meant, even while he loved Danny like nothing else in the world.

At the end of my street, West 93rd, across from the Turin apartment building, there's a gap in the wall along Central Park West, which led to a path that led to two playgrounds. Up top, on a great granite slab, to the right, was the "Hippo Park"; a family of hippopotamuses wallowed in a soft foam lake, made for kids. I'd sit on one hippo while Marshall sat on another larger hippo, the father hippo. It wasn't most people's idea of a great intellectual, sitting on a hippo in a tie dye t-shirt on a summer's morning, in a pair of shorts and sandals. But Marshall wasn't your average great intellectual.

We'd stroll over to the larger play park nearer the street. We'd regularly meet there. Sit on a bench. Talk, say nothing, silence, watch the kids, watch Danny, talk a bit more, talk to Danny, silence again. Marshall sometimes pointed stuff out, pointed across the street, to somebody who once lived in that building over there, to some incident a while back here in the park, when you couldn't walk around after twilight, the "witching hour." To see kids back in the park, he said, was wonderful. He could remember a time when there were no kids. You can't really understand everyday city life, he said, without kids. And you can't understand kids in cities without playgrounds. Kids' playgrounds are one of the most overlooked scenes of cultural life in the city, he said. Grace Paley knew that, he said. More people should read her stories. They're rich with mothers and kids and politics and everyday struggles. A lot unfolds in playgrounds. Some of his happiest moments, Marshall said, have been in playgrounds, with his own kids, seeing other smiling families, moms and pops of all colors and persuasions, talking all kinds of languages, goofing around with their kids. Everything for the kids, for children of the future.

Grace Paley was twenty years Marshall's senior, another Jewish Bronx primitive, daughter of Russian émigré parents, Socialist-Zionists. For years, she lived in Greenwich Village, had "two small boys whose dependence on me takes up my lumpen time and my bourgeois feelings." She was a working mother, an intermittent housewife—"the poorest-paying job a woman can hold"—who got to know another working mother and intermittent housewife, Jane Jacobs. Paley and Jacobs mobilized against Robert Moses building an expressway through Washington Square Park. They won. They protested together, famously got arrested together, in 1967, in an anti-war demo, along with Allen Ginsberg and Susan Sontag.

Paley protested about the lousy state of the city's playgrounds; she wrote stories about those battles with City Hall. "A group of mothers from our neighborhood went downtown to the Board of Estimate Hearing and sang a song," one story, "Politics," began. A mother sang a sad melody learned in her mother's kitchen, a lament requesting better playground facilities. "Oh oh oh / will somebody please put a high fence up / around the children's playground / they are playing a game and have one more year of childhood /...won't the city come / to keep the bums and the tramps out of the yard / they are too little to know the old men wagging their cricked pricks at them." "No one on the Board of Estimate," wrote Paley, "including the mayor, was unimpressed." "By noon the next day, the fence went up."

Paley, like her hero, Isaac Babel, like Raymond Carver—who admired, even envied Paley's writings—was a master of brevity.

Like Carver, she wrote out of necessity short tales rather than long novels, because she never had time to go further. Unlike Carver, she was often working a job *and* looking after the kids; the writing came somewhere in between, "jammed until midnight, with fifteen different jobs and places." The Paley story I like best is "Wants," from the mid-1970s, less than three pages long. I once heard Grace Paley read it aloud, chewing gum, as she did. Gum stopped her from drying out, she said. Each time I've reread "Wants" I *smell* the NY Public Library along Amsterdam Avenue, between West 81st and 82nd Streets; I used to borrow books from there. I used to go with Marshall, who also borrowed books there. He made it a policy to go there, to borrow novels. Shellie, his wife, went there, too; sometimes they went there together, unlike Paley, who, in "Wants," goes to the library alone, yet sees her ex in the street.

"Hello, my life," said Paley. "We had once been married for twenty-seven years, so I felt justified." "He said, "What? No life of mine." "The librarian said $32 even and you've owed it for eighteen years. I didn't deny anything. Because I don't understand how time passes. I had those books. I have often thought of them. The library is only two blocks away." "I gave the librarian a check for $32. Immediately she trusted me, put my past behind her, wiped the record clean, which is just what most other municipal and/or state bureaucracies will *not* do."

The story continued: "I looked through *The House of Mirth*, but lost interest. I want to do something. I want, for instance, to be a different person. I want to be a woman who brings books back in two weeks. I want to be the effective citizen who changes the school system and addresses the Board of Estimate on the troubles of this dear urban center. I wanted to have been married forever to one person, my ex-husband or my present one. Either has enough character for a whole life, which as it turns out is really not such a long time. Just this morning I looked out the window to watch the street for a while and saw that the little sycamores the city had dreamily planted a couple of years before the kids were born had come that day to the prime of their lives."

Marshall loved Grace Paley because of *kids*. I'm not sure they ever met one another. He quoted a Paley line in many pieces he wrote, the same line, over and over again. I guess it spoke to him somehow. It said something about kids, and about his cherished, long lost South Bronx: "*the block is burning down on one side of the street, and the kids are trying to build something on the other.*" Children of the future.

Something weird happened to me that first New York summer. I'm not sure I ever got over it. I was lost someplace else. I'd spend whole afternoons going into Central Park, at "my" entrance at the end of the street, and sit on one of the benches immediately lining the path. There I'd sit and ponder; ponder on what I'm not sure. I'd drift elsewhere, which was very odd because I was sitting in Central Park, in New York City, my backyard now, so why the hell should I be elsewhere and not *here*; it was New York, damn it, pretty fantastic. If I looked over my shoulder I see could see the Eldorado; further down was the San Remo—landmark apartment blocks, figureheads on the Central Park skyline, designed by Emery Roth in the late 1920s and early 1930s. I was sitting in dreamland. Rather a dream come true. I'd realized my dream, my pledge from long ago. There was nothing left to dream about; an ambition achieved. And that's perhaps why I was having this recurrent nightmare, that somebody was going to take it all away, that it was not real. But it was real.

What was I supposed to do when, after a while, this life became normalized, that sitting in Central Park would no longer be surreal? I think that's what I was experiencing then. Reality had kicked in. I couldn't handle that this was now my normal everyday life. Why couldn't I just lighten up and accept it, not think too much about it? Corinna couldn't understand what had come over me. She'd noticed. I was distant from her, no longer intimate, withdrawn and brooding, touchy and bloody difficult to be with. Another Carole King lyric came to mind: "It used to be so easy, livin' here with you. / You were light and breezy, an' I knew just what to do. / Now you look so unhappy, and I feel like a fool."

I started to complain as well, she said, about this and that, about the geeky tax accountant guy upstairs walking too heavily, stomping his feet, tap-dancing on our ceiling all hours. Didn't he ever sleep? Or do any tax accounting? How many people were up there anyway? And the car alarms late at night, and the garbage trucks early morning, and the moron outside our window on his cell phone, talking at great decibels about stock options. We thought there'd be interesting, creative people about in our building. But most were involved in mindless business, reinforcing my thesis that you didn't have to be very smart to make money. Nor work very hard. We had more in common with the doormen and the doormen knew it.

I wasn't nice to be with. Corinna didn't get it. We should be on top of the world, she said; *I* should be on the top of the world, she said. Can't you just be happy and content? Hmm. I wasn't sure. So I sat in the park and watched the squirrels leap about and dogs come up and sniff me and chase the squirrels; joggers passed by, nannies pushed kids in strollers, and I felt cold even though it was stiflingly hot. I felt like I was having a breakdown or something, a breakdown because of a break through. Now I was here and here was all there was. I needed something to worry about. I'd begun to dread having to go back to teach after the summer recess, to leave New York; a dark cloud loomed over me. I'd have to deal with it. I needed someplace to stay in Worcester during the week. And I'd have to drive, lose my parking spot on the street. And what could I write about now?

I wanted to write something about New York. But who hasn't written about New York? How could I possibly say something original, something that hadn't been said before, something new? Lifelong New Yorkers, like Marshall, wrote about New York; I was just off the boat. How could I say something that hadn't already been said? Said by Marshall, by Richard Sennett, by Sharon Zukin, by Michael Sorkin? And all those lovely memoirs by Kate Simon and Alfred Kazin, by Irving Howe and Pete Hamill, and the writings of Grace Paley and Henry Roth and Ralph Ellison and Jane Jacobs and Betty Smith and Esmeralda Santiago, voicing the New York experience, the black experience, the Jewish experience, the Latina experience, the experience of having experience—how could I compete, write something with *no* experience? I was having an existential crisis. I couldn't handle it. I wanted to be a New York intellectual in a town saturated by New York intellectuals. Now I'd arrived, I had to find my own way around.

I sought Marshall's counsel. He knew what I was saying. He believed you could always write something fresh about cities. There was always something else to add; just get to know the place, he said, give it time, settle in, embed yourself in its experience, keep your eyes and ears open, like Baudelaire, learn how to read the "signs in the street" and you'll be okay. Marshall also believed you should write about where you came from. Why not write something about Liverpool? he wondered. Sometimes distance can help, too. The thought made me recoil in horror.

It reminded me of what Marshall once said to one of his CUNY grad students, a young man called Larry, from Pittsburgh, a big, muscular working-class kid, abandoned by alcoholic parents, brought up by impoverished relatives, managing to escape to university on a football scholarship. There, he discovered, quite by accident, that he loved to read, think and dream, and started to commune with romantic poets and idealist philosophers like Hegel. Marshall asked him what he wants to do with his life. He says become a thinker, search for ultimate truth, and, if he succeeds, proclaim it to the world. Marshall is moved by this ambition, having shared it when he was Larry's age. But first Larry has to write a dissertation. On what?

Marshall suggests an ethnographic and political study of his home steel town. Larry's appalled by the idea, tells Marshall that world is crumbling; the mills are shutting down, jobs disappearing, families disintegrating, social networks ripping apart at the seams. When Larry revisits old local bars, men who used to taunt him for loving books and hanging out with kikes, fags, niggers, and commies in New York now envy him for having a lifeline to an outside world. Larry grew up hating this town; hate helped him learn who he was. But it's too much to go back and stare down the abyss again. That's just how I felt, I told Marshall. I wasn't ready to confront Liverpool. Not yet. I'd spent half a lifetime trying to get out. Hating it helped me learn who I was. I was still learning.

For several years, I went back and forth to Worcester. I could do it on autopilot, down to a fine art, one hundred and seventy miles in three hours flat—barring snow and accidents. I knew the route better than the back of my hand, knew every pothole, every place the state cops lay waiting. With my E-ZPass I zoomed through the tolls. I'd leave late Monday evening, sometimes early Tuesday morning, enter onto the West Side Highway (Henry Hudson Parkway) at the 96th Street ramp, cruise up to past the Cloisters, across the Bronx on the Saw Mill River Parkway, then the Cross County Parkway, then the Hutchinson River Parkway, through

Westchester, then the Merritt Parkway through Connecticut, then I-91, past Hartford, then I-84, then I-90, and then, finally, I-290 straight into Worcester. The following Thursday, late afternoon, occasionally Friday lunchtime, I'd return, running the exact same route in reverse, home before supper time. Only one time, one winter, did I think I wasn't going to make it. Late Monday night I got caught in a blizzard. Through Connecticut it got progressively worse. Soon I couldn't see nor drive at speed, had no idea where I was. I was staring at an impenetrable white fog. I thought I'd have to stop, sleep in the car, maybe freeze to death, alone on the highway, firemen digging my icy remains out next morning, reporting back to Corinna the sad news of my tragic, premature demise.

Yet somehow I kept going, held the wheel firm, crawled through the ice and snow, windshield blades working full blast, just about wiping away the snow, tires just about gripping the highway, eventually making it, six hours later, in the middle of the night, greatly relieved. I remember listening to a Germaine Montero CD all the way, her singing old sentimental French songs, written by Pierre Mac Orlan. They inspired me to keep going, to stay alive. Germaine sang about sad, dingy bars, about melancholy old men standing under deserted bridges at midnight, crooning about long, lost lovers, about their cruel fate, about the one that got away. Mac Orlan's stanzas were impregnated with stale beer, with barroom brawls where nobody really got hurt and protagonists, starved for a little bread, love, and a warm bed, had nothing to fear but themselves. I was howling along with Germaine, welling up, moved by the music, by wintry circumstance, by the angelic vision of Corinna's face right there in front of me. Georges Brassens once said, "Mac Orlan's songs give memories to those who don't have any." I thought there and then that these might be my last.

Oddly, Worcester helped for a while. It kept New York special, shuck me out of any complacency I might have had with my adopted home city, any normalizing process. Leaving it made coming back all the more epic, something that would never cease to leave me awestruck, that first tingling glimpse of the Manhattan skyline, the thunderous onslaught of expressways jammed with traffic, its throbbing immensity, a recumbent giant about to swallow me up. Going away for part of the week, during school time, meant New York stayed separate from my university life, free from contamination, from the other existence I had. In Worcester, I was an academic; in New York, a struggling writer, an intellectual, on the fringe, where I belonged. I would forever make my way on the edge, on the periphery, never at the core. Corinna and I always said we were marginal people; we even lived on the margins of our building. We tended not to get on well with things at the core, with "successful" people, with people who didn't have to struggle to keep their lives together.

Wooden townhouses dominated Worcester, especially near campus. Once grand family dwellings were now multi-occupied properties, cheap rentals. A few had been restored. Most were rundown, with busted-up yards out back. Inside, apartments were gloomy and moldy. Floorboards creaked when you stepped on them. Sound traveled between floors, through walls. Screen doors went bam each time someone came and went. Their porches had old sofas whose innards gaped. I rented a room in one house from Jim. Jim came into JB's sometimes, a retired gentleman, soft-spoken, respectable, a Worcester native. He heard I was looking for a place during the week. He said he rented out part of his own townhouse, just around the corner; a room in the top floor apartment was vacant. Real simple. Pay by the week. Only when you're there, he said. No commitments. Seems perfect, I said. Only issue, Jim said, was I'd have to share the apartment with Jerry; own room and all, just the kitchen and bathroom with Jerry, a mature guy, quiet. He'll be no bother, Jim said.

I never saw Jerry by day. He was in bed. I got up early, made coffee in a spartan, musty kitchen, rushed out to a full day teaching. I came back early evening, went to bed, drifted off quickly, purposely had no life. Each night, early hours, I'd be awoken by the house door slamming down below. Then the dull thud of footsteps mounting the stairs. Then another slam, the apartment door. Jerry was back. I'd met him only once before, when Jim introduced us; a big, burly guy, ten years older than me, worn around the edges. Then he'd make himself supper, or perhaps it was breakfast. God knows where he'd been. He'd mooch about half the night. Later, the TV went on, just loud enough to penetrate the white wall receptors of my mind. Sleep was impossible.

I mentioned Jerry's nocturnal habits to Jim. Jim said he'd have a word. Jerry was having a rough time, apparently. Out of work, no woman, bit of a loser. Life hasn't been kind to him, Jim said. Afterward nothing changed with Jerry. He kept coming in late, made the same noises, followed the same pattern. So I told Jim it wasn't going to work out. Jim was real disappointed, seemed he liked the idea of a working professor renting from him. I never saw much of Jim again, it was always awkward when I did at JB's. Maybe he was as embarrassed as I was, stayed away because he knew I was often there. Ever since, wooden houses give me the creeps.

I should have known better, I guess, than to rent another room in a wooden house, in a prof's wooden house this time, a colleague's. She had space, was divorced with two teenage kids, two dogs, and two cats in the Worcester 'burbs. I had the run of the place yet one bathroom was permanently out of use. In it lived Barney, a three-foot long Iguana lizard, shacked up in the bathtub, eyeing you from a large gnarled branch. A small infra-red heater, always on, lay beside him, bringing tropical warmth to freezing Worcester. Barney was a scary sight. Each night I'd check in on him, ensure his bathroom door was *firmly* shut.

On the surface, life here appeared normal. But really it was a dysfunctional mess. People say New Yorkers are fucked up; it always struck me that crazy New Yorkers were saner than the rest of America. Life's hang-ups were more out in the open, more public in New York, not repressed behind closed shutters and drawn curtains. It was like Spalding Gray said. You could go out in the street in New York and start yelling your head off. Nobody would think it weird. If anything, they'd start yelling with you. In Worcester, the yells were quiet sobs of private desperation.

Nobody ever used the kitchen. My colleague had given up cooking long ago, after her marriage failed. She'd given up the traditional motherly thing, with a partner, and a straight life. I never knew where or what her kids ate. I was the only person who cooked anything. They were never there. The dining table never featured as a dining table. Accumulated junk and piled up papers commandeered it. Dogs roamed the house, had free rein, leaving their hairs everywhere. Cats napped in the kitchen, lolled about on the table, on work tops, on window ledges, likewise leaving their hairs everywhere. One time, getting in late from New York, exhausted, going up to my room, I found a large turd in the center of the floor, dry but still smelly, left the previous weekend by one of the dogs, a welcome back gift. The room stank for ages afterward. In bleak mid-winter, I had to keep the windows wide open.

My colleague snacked on whatever, hardly ever exited her bedroom, where she read voraciously, and drank, tippled liquor quietly, to her solitary heart's content. She had a drink problem and she knew it. Her son was a lost soul, smart yet flunking high school, depressed a lot of the time, couldn't see the point about life, about the future, not yet sixteen. My colleague's maternal ambition was to see her kids make it alive through adolescence, until they were old enough to fend for themselves. The bar was set that low in terms of her expectations. I tried to communicate with the son. He always wore black, had unkempt, thick curly black hair, wore punk garb. I spoke to him about punk rock, which I knew first time around. It was my generation. The year I quit high school, 1976, the Sex Pistols' *Anarchy in the UK* was released. "I wanna destroy, what's the point!" Johnny Rotten had bawled. The Sex Pistols' mantra of "NO FUTURE" seemed just about right then, my era's manifesto.

Somehow, I said, I found a way to create a future for myself, to emerge out of the void, doing it through books, my lifeline.

I told the son he should check out Greil Marcus's *Lipstick Traces*, a fun book charting the lineage between punk rock and past avant-garde anarchist movements, like Dada and the Situationists, the latter fronted by Guy Debord. I said he might find this story interesting, even inspiring; I had, when I wasn't much older than him. We never spoke about it again. I'm not sure he ever made it to *Lipstick Traces*. Years later, after I'd left Worcester, left New York, left America, I heard he'd killed himself, strung himself up from a tree in the backyard. He'd made it through adolescence. But demons continued to haunt him into young adulthood.

Every Thursday, a triumphant homecoming, Ulysses returning to Ithaca, exhilarated to be back in the city, to feel terra firma underfoot, solid granite after so much creaking wood. It was thrilling to park the car. I would drive for three hours and then spend another hour circling blocks of the Upper West Side, hunting for the "right" parking spot, on the "right" side of the street. The walk back to my apartment was especially joyous. A band struck up in my head. No matter how tired I felt, I always had a spring in my step, inhaling that familiar odor of the Upper West Side, feeling again a universe full of people, with street lights and sidewalks. Early evening, suppertime, on this island Earth.

Corinna was always relieved to see me. But I'd not linger. I had a set program Thursday nights. I needed to decompress, re-acclimate, do it on my own. Corinna always said it reflected something about my personality, about the frequent need to get my head together by myself. We had tried going out. But it never worked. We'd start arguing about something petty. I was too psyched about returning, a bit too self-absorbed, high from the car ride. I needed to clear out by myself. So I'd go out almost immediately, dumping my bags, swilling my face, then walking up near Columbia University to have supper at a cheap pasta joint called Café Pertutti, between West 112th and 113th Streets, one of the best-valued Italian restaurants in Manhattan.

It was amongst Marshall's favorites; he'd introduced me to it early on. We'd met there on a Saturday night, me and Corinna, Marshall and Shellie and Danny and Eli, Marshall's eldest son. The owner knew Marshall and a made a nice fuss, moving around tables and chairs to accommodate us all as a group. I liked the welcoming atmosphere, its no-nonsense feel. I could see why Marshall liked it. Thereafter I went to Pertutti often, ate the same thing each Thursday, avocado and bacon salad for starters, a big bowl, then a pasta dish, hearty portion, guzzled down with a carafe of cheap red wine, always tasting like nectar those Thursday evenings. Its moderate price seemed a minor miracle.

It made everything taste better than it was. Always the place was bustling. Always I dug its busyness without pretense. What a loss its closing, priced out of the neighborhood in 2008.

Clanging plates and loud chatter were all right those Pertutti nights. I was so high to be back in New York that I sucked in pure atmosphere. Everything seemed sacramental, a gift, an act to venerate, pouring myself another glass of wine, scooping up the last dregs of salad, bits of bacon and vinaigrette, with a morsel of bread, surveying the clientele. Noises and images, thoughts and faces. Everything appeared before me with cosmic lucidity. I could penetrate the absolute reality of the Kantian noumenon, the thing in itself, without any mediation of the phenomenon. I could hear aloud people thinking. All felt "holy" in the way Allen Ginsberg incanted in his footnote to *Howl*: "Everything is holy! everybody's holy! everywhere is holy! everyday is in eternity! Everyman's an angel! ... Holy the solitudes of skyscrapers and pavements! Holy the cafeterias filled with the millions! Holy the mysterious rivers of tears under the streets! ... Holy New York ..."

I got tipsy those evenings. Moderate drunkenness always made for a magnificent and comforting peace. All is well, that's what it was saying to me: all is well. I'd totter out of Pertutti after my meal, feeling a satiated happiness, a warm fulfillment. I could have walked a dead straight line but it felt better tottering. I wanted to totter. Afterward I'd spend a good while next door at the international news store, browsing its magazines and newspapers, going through all sections—politics and design, architecture and cinema, cultural studies and current affairs, scrutinizing the international press, the British press, the French press, reading stuff I would never feel the need to read again and now no longer want to read. Yet those nights I needed to know everything, could absorb everything. At least it seemed I could. "You must know everything," Isaac Babel had written in one of his stories. "'Your grandfather was ruled by an insatiable thirst for knowledge and life. Study!' my grandmother suddenly said with great vehemence, 'study and you will have everything—wealth and fame! You must know *everything*. The whole world will fall at your feet and grovel before you.'"

The whole world was groveling before me those magical Thursday homecoming evenings, when I'd stagger down Broadway, giving my loose change away to panhandlers, to anybody who approached me on the street, fearless, munching on a York Peppermint Pattie bought for dessert at a deli. Onwards to 93rd Street. Corinna would be tucked up in bed watching TV by then. We'd cuddle up together, in front of another *Law & Order* rerun, confessing our love of Jerry Orbach, hard-bitten Detective Lennie Briscoe.

New York's on-street parking regulations never ceased to amaze me; that you could park your car on many streets without paying, without filling the meter, without getting ripped off by charges. But you had to take care in this strange democracy, with its own social contract. Those regulations were challenging, a complex highway code unto themselves. I once learned a lesson the hard way, coming down from Boston for a long weekend, parking on Riverside Drive one Friday night, only to find the car gone Monday afternoon when I returned. At first, I'd thought it had been stolen. But who would steal such a thing? Then a passerby, an elderly man, saw our distress. We explained what had happened, that the car had seemingly disappeared, but where? The pound, he'd said, shaking his head. You left it in a bus stop, see, between those red arrows, on the signs above. Red arrows and "NO STANDING ANYTIME." It's a bus stop. You can't park at a bus stop, he said. The pound, that's where it'll be, over near Port Authority.

Sure enough, the NYPD's Traffic Enforcement Division had confiscated the car, taken it to the tow pound, Pier 76 at West 38th Street and 12th Avenue. A tow truck had come to cart it away. It cost me nearly a thousand bucks to retrieve it, from dark Hell's Kitchen, like a scene from a gangster movie, with rundown warehouses and piers and shady looking mobsters hanging around. And they were just the cops. But I knew thereafter that reading the signs in the street, in bright red, announcing "NO STANDING," really meant NO STANDING. It took time before you learned how to decipher the dazzling array of street signage on the sidewalk, greeting New York motorists. You can't park at a designated bus stop, that I now knew, nor within a fire hydrant zone, nor double-park, nor leave it too long at an unpaid parking meter.

The trickiest of all was Alternate-Side Parking (ASP), for street-cleaning. That's what I meant by finding the "right" spot, on the "right" side of the street, nabbing it quickly, ensuring you get as long as possible before leaving, before having to move again for the next street-cleaning day. ASP governs the Upper West Side. If you're gonna leave your car on any of its streets you had to negotiate this law of the land. Broadway, to be avoided, because it's metered-parking only, and not what you want. Metered-parking is for shoppers, not residents. Instead, you stuck to the streets, or to Riverside Drive and Central Park West, always good bets for finding the right spot. ASP comes with its own red-signed warnings. Between those hours, on those days, you had to get your car off that side of street. The street-sweeper had to pass. Up and down and across, between 86th and 96th Streets, Riverside Park and Central Park, ASP prevailed. This was my zone of engagement.

I'd learn its timetable by heart. Gradually, you became a driving Parkopedia.

Some sides of the street were street-cleaning 8:30–10 AM TUES & THURS; others 11:30 AM TO 1 PM MON & FRI; still more 8-9 AM MON & FRI, all flagged up with a large red "P" inside a circle with a crossed broom through it. If I arrived back from Worcester early Thursday evening, last thing I wanted was to park in a spot marked 8–9 AM MON & FRI. Next morning, Friday, I'd not get to sleep in, would have get up, bright and early, before eight, to move the car someplace else, maybe, if I got lucky, across the street, or double-park the same spot and wait in the car. You got excited if you saw a great spot on the street, a "good till Monday" space. That was the Holy Grail: 8:30–10 AM TUES & THURS. Then I could abandon the car until I left the following Monday evening, since I had avoided street-cleaning that previous morning and the next one wasn't until Tuesday, when I'd be long gone, up in Worcester.

Double-parking was illegal yet tolerated, often necessary. Before long, you'd join in yourself and double-park on street-cleaning days. You'd shift your car over from the sidewalk, create a car's width space, and stay put until the street-sweeper trundled through on your near side. Afterward you'd simply re-park where you'd been before. No telling exactly when the street-sweeper would come. So you had to sit tight, take something to read, hold your ground, watch out for patrolling cop cars. If the mood took them, they could ticket you. Ahead and behind you'd find others doing likewise, double-parking, similarly on the lookout, scanning a *New York Post* or *Daily News*. During school vacation, when I was permanently in the city, I had to remember to re-park the car. It was often a pain. ASP suspensions, at state or national holidays, came as blissful relief.

Sometimes if you saw an opening, you had to *create* your own parking space, learning how to maneuver your car in tight spaces, parking in spaces even smaller than the car itself. You had to make those spaces larger than they were, bumping the fenders of cars ahead and behind you, rocking them gently, shifting them forward or backward, pushing and shoving, advancing and reversing, nudging adjacent cars to make way for your own. It was the unwritten law of the streets, acceptable behavior—up to a point. Everybody did it. Cars with unblemished fenders were out of town cars.

Someone once ripped my front fender off trying to get in a tight spot. He got tangled up with my car, went too hard, too fast or too clumsily, reversing and advancing, dragging my fender with him. He'd violated those unwritten laws, gone beyond reasonable bumping. Unusually, I had parked on my own street and our doorman, Angel, witnessed it all, ran out hollering, *yo, fella, watch that car!* Angel got his license plate, his name and telephone number, then came legging back to tell me, ringing my door bell. It took the culprit a while before he coughed up the three hundred and fifty dollars to have the fender repaired. To begin with, he tried to deny it. But we had a witness. Eventually, he agreed to settle privately, without any insurance claim. He paid me in two installments, cash. I didn't want any check. Bizarrely, he'd cried poverty, although he said he was some kind of lawyer. He was one of the many jerks of the Upper West Side.

Doormen are the wily "eyes on the street" that Jane Jacobs talked about, neighborhood safety patrols. They knew a thing or two about what was happening on the block, almost everything in fact, recognized most of the parked cars, whose cars they were, where the owners lived. If you got on your doorman's good side, gave them a nice Xmas tip, or slipped them the odd twenty-dollar bill, they'd re-park for you sometimes, and look out for good spots coming free. Though they kept the best spots for themselves, made sure they got the best spots. Doormen in other buildings did likewise. They all knew one another, pooled knowledge. Whole blocks operated to this hidden dynamic, invisible to the unknowing, to anybody who underestimated the power of a doorman's street knowledge.

I never thought parking would ever figure in my urban imaginary. I found myself talking about it at social gatherings, sharing tales of the joys and dreads of parking your car. People with cars experienced the same frustrations, the same victories, the same highs and lows, finding a great space, not finding the right space. Before I moved to New York, I never knew any of this. It bored Corinna when I spoke about it; how could it not. She never drove, never had to park the car. It was hard for anybody who didn't drive to get it, to understand the camaraderie and rivalry that seasoned New York motorists held for other seasoned New York motorists, cruising the streets in search of that beautiful spot. Corinna wondered what was happening to me, a redoubtable "foot person." All this car talk, she said. I told her that parking became compelling *because* I was a foot person. Once the car was tucked up someplace safe, I was free, could pace the streets again uninhibited, with clear conscience, liberated from the anxiety of having to re-park. For a while.

One of the great ironies of journeying to and fro between New York and Worcester was *Robert Moses*, how he'd facilitated it. None of my trip would have ever been conceivable, let alone possible, without Moses's dirty work. Almost everything my wheels touched in the New York region—every expressway, parkway, bridge, and tunnel—bore the notorious Park Commissioner's

Faustian spell, blasting, bulldozing, and bullying his way through New York's cityscape from the 1950s onwards. "When you operate in an overbuilt metropolis," Moses liked to boast, "you had to hack your way with a meat ax." None of this was lost on Marshall, of course. I mentioned my Moses car paradox to him. I was defensive about it because I knew how he hated Moses; anyone who has read the final chapter of *All That Is Solid* would know this.

Marshall had learned how to drive but didn't own a car. I imagined him sometimes at the wheel like Woody Allen's Alvy in *Annie Hall*, on his LA trip, allergic to automobiles, skidding and stalling and crashing into other cars, releasing his repressed Moses anger as if riding a Coney Island dodgem. Oh how Marshall would have loved to run Moses down! Moses was a horrible man who did horrible things yet Marshall's hatred was never straightforward. He spent a lifetime wrestling with Moses's troubling ambiguities and contradictions. "In the spring and fall of 1953, Moses began to loom over my life," Marshall wrote in *All That Is Solid*. "Moses proclaimed that he was to ram an immense expressway, unprecedented in scale, expense and difficulty of construction, through our neighbourhood's heart. At first we couldn't believe it; it seemed to come from another world... hardly any of us owned cars: the neighborhood itself, and the subways leading downtown, defined the flow of our lives."

"I can remember standing above the construction site of the Cross Bronx Expressway," Marshall said, "weeping for my neighborhood. The Grand Concourse, from whose heights I watched and thought, was our borough's closest thing to a Parisian boulevard. Among its most striking features were rows of large, splendid 1930s apartment houses. As I saw one of the loveliest of these building being wrecked for the road, I felt a grief that, I can see now, is endemic to modern life. So often the price of an ongoing and expanding modernity is the destruction not merely of 'traditional' and 'pre-modern' institutions and environments but—and here is the real tragedy—of everything most vital and beautiful in the modern world itself. Here in the Bronx, thanks to Robert Moses, the modernity of the urban boulevard was being condemned as obsolete, and blown to pieces, by the modernity of the interstate highway." "To be modern," Marshall rued, "turned out to be far more problematical, and more perilous, than I had been taught."

A few years before he wrote *All That Is Solid Melts into Air*, Marshall reviewed, in the now-defunct indie magazine *Ramparts*, Robert Caro's whopping great Moses bio, *The Power Broker*. Caro was a man who hated Moses even more than Marshall did. Still, Marshall warned of the dangers of obsessional hatred: Caro frothing at the mouth, with manic rage, was a sort of overkill, ruthlessly dealing with Moses as Moses had ruthlessly dealt with people. Steady on, said Marshall. Didn't Moses come to embody the New Deal optimism of the postwar period, even the optimism of postwar America itself? (*On the Road*, remember, was a book of Moses's generation.) And didn't Moses embody the same developmental forces that Marx praised in *The Communist Manifesto*?

The bourgeoisie has "accomplished wonders" of construction, the first part of the *Manifesto* reminded us. It has built Gothic cathedrals, mighty bridges and aqueducts, moved entire mountains, doing it all if it can reap an adequate enough return. It has been "the first to show what man's activity can bring about." In that sense, Marx said, the bourgeoisie has been truly revolutionary. "One of the crucial forces that made bourgeois society go," Marshall claimed, reaffirming Marx, "and generated some of its most brilliant achievements, was its innate drive to 'establish connections everywhere.' However, few bourgeoisie had the imagination to think of this. What made Robert Moses so special was the largeness of his visions and ideas, his intellectual and organizational power to grasp the whole." It's "ironic," Marshall mused, "that this vision, so dear to Marx, should be a lot closer in spirit to Moses, who claimed to hate everything Marx stood for, than to the New Left, which burnt endless candles at Marx's shrine. But if Karl Marx and Robert Moses can share a vision of life that we reject or ignore, we had better find out fast what we are missing."

True enough, Moses forged a New York open and whole. You could witness this immense wholeness in motion, in a car, grasp it, drive through it, watch its giant panorama unfold. The entire city-region hung together, was brought together, much as Haussmann, a century before, had blasted and bullied his way through Paris, stitching it together, forcing neighborhoods to see one another, to confront the explosive forces that would now both unite and threaten them. Marshall knew this, was brave enough to acknowledge it, to think through its troubling logic. "Moses," he said, "took a tremendous and teeming city that developed spontaneously and planlessly from a multitude of isolated villages and separate and insular neighborhoods and dead-end streets—took it all and tied it together." "Slide into the gentle curve of the West Side Highway, and the lights and towers of Manhattan flash and glow before you like a vision, rising above the lush greenness of Riverside Park, and even the most embattled ex- and anti-New Yorker will be touched; you know you have come home again, and you can thank Robert Moses for that."

It was something about what Alfred Kazin called "the block and beyond," an inside-outside affair. When on the outside, beyond

New York, I grew even more attached to the inside, missed it, romanticized it, reimagined it as myth. Back on the inside, I knew there was something more, that there were other insides, that the city was bigger than this, bigger than me, bigger than the city itself. I was glad I could see beyond because it made me a non-complacent New Yorker, kept me apart from the provincial New Yorkers I saw around me, who never left the island, never left their neighborhood, forgetting all about the beyond. Negotiating this inside and outside, this block and beyond, made you not merely a city dweller but metropolitan. It was a way of seeing as well as living in the city. Although, sometimes, I felt I needed more local; that I maybe knew about the beyond at the expense of the block. I needed to know more about what was immediately around me, the city that directly enveloped me. I needed to talk about this for a while.

One block down from my apartment, along Columbus Avenue, I often walked past an enigmatic mural, on the wall of the Goddard Riverside Community Center: two outstretched hands, reaching out to one another, one yellow, the other brown, just about clasping, just about making contact, overlapping at their fingertips. I had often wondered what went on inside this building with this mural. So, one day, in passing, I plucked up the courage to enter and ask. Inside, flyers festooned a noticeboard: "SRO

TENANTS UNITED!"; "SROTU PLANS NEW OUTREACH CAMPAIGN!"; "ORGANIZE FOR ACTION." Phones rang in a cramped, ground-floor office; staff, wearing red T-shirts, hurried by busily, documents under arm. Nobody seemed to notice me, was bothered by my loitering. I'd entered a hive of activity: the West Side's "Law Project," a non-profit organization, conceived, I'd soon discover, in the early 1980s, there to ward off the alarming decline of Single-Room-Occupancy (SRO) housing on the Upper West Side.

SROs have been one of New York's most vital reserves of affordable housing. Manhattan had more than three-quarters of the city's stock, many in large, pre-war apartment hotels. They were all around the Upper West Side if you looked closely at tattier buildings. SROs date back to World War I, when ex-servicemen with no families found a grubby haven. The stock provided cheap and safe shelter for single women, for struggling artists and writers, for factory workers and anyone else who sought work and/or the city's bright lights. Residents inhabited a single room, with meager furniture, sharing a bathroom and kitchen with fellow occupants along the hall. Some of Manhattan's landmark buildings, like the Chelsea Hotel, had, still have, SRO units, rooms for quirky or completely normal poorer clientele who came to New York and never wanted to leave.

SRO tenants have had rights under New York's Rent Stabilization Code. But there are loopholes and landlords always know how to wangle loopholes. Hotel and rooming-house owners can legally charge what they want for the first six months of tenancy. Thereafter, rent is supposed to be lowered to the stabilized level, and residents effectively become "permanent." But so long as SRO tenants remain in the dark about this law, landlords can—and do—charge what they like. The Code, meanwhile, required landlords to provide a tenant with a "Notice of Rights and Duties," a formal contract detailing the precise status of their permanent tenancy, safeguarding them from illegal eviction. Rarely did this happen. Enter the Law Project.

I remember telling the Law Project people something I was always coy about: that I was a "writer"—as if it were a real profession and I a real professional; nothing could be further from the truth. I said I lived nearby, and could I talk to somebody about their work, about SROs, about the Upper West Side? They said come back in a few days and talk to Terry, one of our tenant organizers. I did. Terry was a fifty-something burly man, softly spoken, originally from Louisiana. He had lived in New York for years, was a Sixties student activist and now agitated around housing, helping organize SRO tenants to organize themselves. On the Upper West Side, especially, he said, owners want to convert their

SRO buildings into glitzy condos or "boutique" hotels. En route, a lot of tenants have had their heating and hot water cut, their elevator service disrupted, and been strong-armed by thugs and drug dealers—who, Terry said, were recruited to rid buildings of rent stabilized tenants. If I wanted to know more, he said, I should go talk to some tenants.

Overlooking Broadway is 222 West 77th Street, a big pre-war building, a stone's throw from the Beacon Theatre. Number 222's fortunes mirror the changing fortunes of the Upper West Side, even the changing fortunes of New York itself. In 1976, the building, known as the Benjamin Franklin Hotel, was a shabby residential hotel, full of single-room occupants, working people just about making it. In the 1980s, the SRO was renamed the Broadway American. In the late 1990s, after a costly face-lift and rehab, the old Broadway American was repackaged as On The Avenue Hotel, a mid-priced, short-stay boutique property. A few years back, the building had yet another overhaul and makeover, relaunching itself as the upgraded NYLO, run by a Texas hotel chain, currently offering "4-star accommodation."

Leah, in her sixties, was one of seventy or so remaining SRO tenants at the hotel. I met her in her prim, eighth-floor, oblong room, measuring about fifteen by eight feet. It was decorated with floral curtains. Her divan bed acted as a sofa by day. As we sipped ice tea and talked, Leah's neighbor, Grace, ten years Leah's junior, joined us. "We've had a lot of different owners," Leah told me. "But when I first moved into the building, one elderly gentleman owned it. You had to be interviewed to make sure you were respectable and took care of yourself." She said the neighborhood was frayed and the building shabby—but safe and clean. "It was a little oasis of peace and safety and tranquility. It was a godsend, a lifesaver for me."

Grace arrived in 1981 and paid more. But with a steady bank-telling job it was affordable. Her room, I later discovered, was bright and cheery, twice the size of Leah's, full of plants, with a lovely bird's-eye view over Broadway. "The place was shabby," said Grace, "but very clean and quiet and there was always somebody down at the desk. If they didn't know you, they'd stop you, ask you who you were and where you were going." "Unfortunately," Leah said, "the building started to get run down." After the old owner died, the new one "kept breaking the bathroom windows in the winter. We'd put cardboard up and they'd rip it down. We'd never have heat or hot water." "It was bleak," she said. "They eventually had their license taken away and could no longer operate."

Later in the 1980s, another landlord took control. "They wanted to sell and wanted us out," Leah said. "They wanted richer people in. But we told them we weren't moving, that we had no place else to go. So they started putting in prostitutes and drug dealers and dangerous people, began using terror tactics. Amsterdam Avenue wasn't that safe, neither was Columbus, especially after dark." Leah said that things in and around the building weren't very nice. "The point was that it wasn't supposed to be so nice. We were supposed to leave!"

As they stayed put, the environment around them became tonier. Up and down Broadway, between 72nd and 112th Streets, former SRO buildings were picked off. "It was a neighborhood once," Grace said. "Now, it's all yuppie-duppie. I always felt that when I went outside I was walking with people who were like me, who were just getting the rent check written every month. Now, when you go out you know it's not like that. You feel like you're an outsider. It's so money oriented. If it was before, you didn't feel it. It's another world out there now." "Sometimes," said Leah, "you feel like you're on Fifth Avenue. It's become so posh." Being an SRO tenant once meant independence, Leah lamented. "It was wonderful. This used to be a residential neighborhood. It was our home and they're taking it away."

A week or so on, at Terry's urging, I ventured further north. It was a sultry July morning. I sat on a low wall outside a three-story brownstone on West 120th Street, near Mount Morris Park, in Harlem. Four workmen, covered in dust and dirt, came and went, throwing debris and masonry into a nearby dumpster. They disappeared into a gutted building, number seventeen. From my perch, I could hear drilling and banging inside. My eyes followed a uniform row of red brick and terracotta houses, most built around 1890, grand in their day; many were burnt-out shells, boarded up and abandoned. Wire fences sealed several off; knee-high weeds and accumulated litter made everything feel forlorn and menacing. I watched a disheveled black man, bearing two loaded bags, emerge from one ruin across the street.

As I pondered the scene, looking more closely at the detail, I noticed amid the wreckage and dereliction that a few structures looked healthy. They had fine wooden shutters and renovated facades, recent paint jobs, and window boxes bearing fresh flowers. These new rehabs looked quite delightful, telltale signs of change in the air, that things were getting spruced up and that money was flowing back after decades of flowing out. I was early that morning, for an appointment with number seventeen's last tenant. Incredible that someone was still there, living in what looked like rubble, in a war zone. The workmen couldn't care less when I walked in and went up the stairs in the half-light. The air was thick with dust. I felt it catch my throat. At the top, knocking on a door, a diminutive woman, Mary, greeted me, shaking my hand cheerily, ushering me into a twelve by twelve foot room, filled with her modest possessions: a little TV, a radio, mini-fridge, clothes piled on a single bed, all covered with plastic wrappings—"to protect everything from water leaks and mess," Mary said. In one corner was a cheap bookshelf, upon which lay Alex Haley's *Roots*, a biography of Malcolm X, several Bibles, a bulky bio of Queen Elizabeth II, and, curiously, a paperback *The Art of the Deal* by a certain Donald Trump.

Mary had a mop of black curly hair, with only a couple of gray strands. She said she was fifty-four yet looked ten years younger. She moved to New York aged seven, with her longshoreman father, mother and four siblings, migrating from rural South Carolina. They were poor, moved about a lot at first, several times in Harlem, then to Brooklyn, always into crummy apartments. "We had a lot of rats," Mary said. "There are a lot of bad buildings in New York City." She returned to Harlem in her late teens and has been here, by herself, ever since. "I was living at 121st Street," she said, "until the owner died and the new one started tearing everything down around me." She wanted Mary out. At first, Mary refused to budge. Then the owner began "doing harassment." Mary didn't want trouble. She finally gave in and fled. "I wasn't real happy but a neighborhood friend of mine found me this room. There was nothing better."

After that owner died, things started to deteriorate. The latest landlord, a local entrepreneur, had big plans for his Harlem property. Its eleven units were to be renovated, adjoining walls knocked down on every floor, rooms combined, and new toilets and kitchens installed, transforming dingy rooms into plush one- and two-bedroom apartments. Mary had to scram. "It was a Sunday morning, around seven-thirty. No warning, no letter, no nothing, just 'boom, boom, boom' at the door." Three mighty fellows stood there and gave Mary a week's notice. Overnight, the other tenants left, leaving Mary alone, "walking in wilderness," she said, "the last leaf on a lonely tree. I hope that if the wind blows me off, it blows me to someplace special."

"The drilling and banging lasts all night," she said. The workmen are busy around the clock, came in the morning, left practically at dawn. She couldn't sleep. "I can't do nothing. They got paint in the bathtub. The toilet is all blocked up and doesn't flush. They even took the toilet seat away. Now I have to go to the store around the corner where they have a bathroom." Not long ago the ceiling of her kitchenette, about the size of small closet, caved in. Workers were in the apartment above. There were loud bangs and vibrations and then, suddenly, water came gushing through the light fixture, drenching everything. She had to phone the fire department who turned off the water mains and electricity. "Didn't have either all weekend."

Mary encouraged me to see for myself. I peered into a little alcove, saw an old, grease-stained cooker, and a badly cracked, yellowing ceiling, with a bare lightbulb. "There was a rat running around as well," she said. "Came through a hole in the kitchen, like a little kitten. I started walkin' 'round in boots. I was too scared to even eat and sleep. I could hear him moving around like a human being." It was then that Mary accused her landlord of harassment. She started to act. Harlem's legal services on 125th Street recommended she consult the West Side SRO Law Project. Mary didn't waste any time. "They have been very effective at trying to help me."

"We can only try to stop the floodgates from opening," Terry told me when we met up again, "force landlords to retain some rooms for permanent residents while allowing them to convert others for richer folk." This was as good as it got for the foreseeable future. Many displaced tenants will doubtless go and live with family or friends, if they have any; some, if they're lucky, may find alternative cheap housing; many more will end up in shelters; and a few will find their way onto the streets. One day, Terry and his colleagues hoped for real political commitment toward affordable, single-person accommodation, probably not SROs but studio apartments with kitchenettes and bathrooms. For the time being, "we don't see any commitment to a program that benefits poor, working class people in this city."

As I exited the Law Project's offices, on my way home, I remember being thankful that I had a home, not a single room but two rooms—or a single room divided into two, clean and safe. I glanced again at that mural, those two almost-clasping hands. Then I thought of Mary, sitting in her little Harlem room, amid the rubble, wondering where she might go next, thinking about whose hand she might clasp. Something she said lingered with me. She'd cited from her Bible, 2 Kings 7:3, the parable of the "lepers at the city gate." Four leprous men deliberate. "Why should we sit here until we die? If we decide to go into the city, we shall die there, for there is famine in the city. If we remain here, we shall die too." The lepers have really nothing to lose, sort of like Mary. So they decide to go to the camp of the Aramaeans. If they spare us, we live; if they kill us, we die." The lepers can't know the outcome in advance. As it happens, when the men reach the camp, no one is there. They eat, drink, and clothe themselves. Their activism somehow saved them: it would have saved them even if they'd lost. Mary found inspiration here: "I, too, am entering the city," she'd said. "We SRO tenants are lepers at the city gate of New York. Why should we sit here and die?"

For as long as I can remember, I've identified with lepers. I know this sounds arch but I've always felt more connected to outsiders, to peripheral people, to lepers, than to rich insiders, to people who define the inside and outside. I've often wondered whether hailing from Liverpool made me more sympathetic to the hard done by, to the stigmatized, to residues who are left out. It seems these days that more and more people are residual in our urban system. They aren't so much remainders in the city as the very substance of cities themselves, that there are more people left out in big cities than counted in.

I once wrote a book about donkeys, years ago now, and somebody asked me why I wanted to do a strange thing like that. I said I couldn't write about horses because horses were haughty and proud whereas donkeys were horses who hadn't succeeded. I'm not sure the person was satisfied with my answer. But I never wanted into the inside. That was my peculiar privilege: an outsider by choice. I came to New York because I wanted to live in a neighborhood, a cosmopolitan neighborhood, where I thought I could belong to the block and beyond. The block was big enough to let me grow, to express myself, to do it with Corinna, to express ourselves together, to grow old together. It was big enough to ignore us, to let us be. But when I thought about it, my coming was part of the destruction of the neighborhood; my type, with connections to a bigger beyond, was precisely the same force that destroyed SRO buildings. Whether I liked it or not, I was the yuppie-duppie Grace spoke about. This was always very troubling for me, almost as troubling, perhaps, as Robert Moses was for Marshall.

Even when I walked around the Upper West Side, admiring buildings like the San Remo or Eldorado or Emery Roth's other fantasy structure, the Beresford, facing the Natural History Museum at 81st Street—or the full-block Belnord on West 86th Street, where I. B. Singer lived, or the frayed grandiosity of the Apthorp, the world's largest apartment building in 1908, at 79th Street, where I suspect the reclusive writer Thomas Pynchon lives—I knew these places weren't for the likes of me and Corinna. They were somehow the inside, both physically and existentially, with inner courtyards protecting them from the outside. Even inside our apartment, we were practically on the outside.

Sometimes, I strolled down Central Park West, surveying the wonderful apartment buildings that face the park. It was my neighborhood yet another world. I'd frequently stop at 72nd Street, linger longer, looking at the daddy apartment of them all, the Dakota building. In the late 1870s, when millionaire businessman Edward Clark proposed to build the grandest apartment complex ever, on the park at 72nd, people thought him mad. There was nothing around then. The place was so desolate they said Clark might as well build it in Dakota. Pioneering Clark was smitten by the idea, used the label ironically, and decorated the Dakota's high wall above its entrance with a terracotta portrait of a Native American chief. Inside, apartments had columned rooms up to fifty-feet long, with fourteen-foot ceilings, three-foot thick walls, floors of oak, cherry, hazelwood and mahogany, palatial dining rooms with marble underfoot and hand-carved paneling and stairwells. Movie stars like Lauren Bacall later lived there.

On the outside, fortress-like, with its somber dark-brown brick, the Dakota looked intimidating. When you stood directly outside it, under it, it seemed out of reach, a castle straight out of Kafka's *The Castle*. There but not there. Its occupants never seemed at home, shutters always shut. The large gap between the building and the street felt like a moat whose drawbridge never dropped. You had to crane your neck to look at even the ground-floor apartments. I often wondered how it felt for the Liverpudlian who once lived there, John Lennon, an insider who I never really saw as an insider. Maybe he was a Trojan Horse insider. With wife Yoko Ono (and son Sean), he commandeered twenty-nine rooms on the seventh-floor, buying up adjoining apartments. Residents initially resisted their coming, fearing raucous parties and the couple's unconventional lifestyle, loud amplified music.

Lennon had just fled Britain, married Yoko Ono (in Gibraltar in 1969), split with the Beatles (1970), had a heroin bust, a criminal record, was a political undesirable. His FBI file grew. The US State Department didn't want him in. Yet in 1972, they let him in. Soon Lennon got himself a Green Card and they couldn't throw him out. He settled down as a Dakota dad. For almost a decade, the Lennons kept to themselves, wanting privacy rather than limelight. Sometimes, in crazy disguise, John ventured out into New York. Amongst other crazy eccentrics, nobody recognized him, nor seemingly cared. Then, late Monday evening, December 8, 1980, returning without disguise with Yoko from the Hit Factory recording studio, making music again, Mark David Chapman took out a .38 revolver outside the Dakota's entrance and shot Lennon dead. The former Beatle hadn't long turned forty.

John said he was glad to get out of Liverpool; there was never any love lost; I got what he meant, but have lived longer than him. Where you come from matters more as you get older. In a series of interviews John did for *Rolling Stone* back in 1970, not long after the Beatles broke up, Jann Wenner asked him what was Liverpool like? What did Liverpool mean to John Lennon? At first, John was a bit diffident, unusually reticent. "Liverpool was just where I was brought up," he said. "It's like anywhere." Wenner, not entirely convinced by the response, pushed Lennon more. "What did being from Liverpool have to do with your art?" Wenner wondered.

"Because it was a port," John got going, soon hitting his stride, "that means it was *less* hick than somewhere in the midlands, like the Midwest or whatever you call it. We were a port, the second biggest in England. Also between Manchester and Liverpool, the North was where all the money was made in the 1880s whenever it was, that was where all the brass and the heavy people were. And that's where the despised people were. We were the ones that were looked *down* upon by the southerners as *animals*... [Liverpool] was a very poor city and tough. But people had a sense of humor because they're in so much pain. So they're always cracking jokes, they're very witty. And it's an Irish place. It's where the Irish came when they ran out of potatoes. And it's where black people were left or worked as slaves or whatever and the trader communities. It's cosmopolitan, and it's where the sailors would come home with blues records from America on the ships! And the biggest country & western following in England is in Liverpool. I remember the first guitar I ever saw was a guy's in a cowboy suit in Liverpool with the stars and the cowboy hat. And a big dobro. They're real cowboys there, they take it seriously. There've been cowboys long before there was rock & roll. There's folk clubs and all that was going on there. So there's all that kind of environment."

On a wall of one of Lennon's Dakota apartment corridors was a painting he'd done, aged eleven, at Liverpool's Dovedale Primary School. He'd kept it into adulthood, was meaningful to him. In another life, I've walked past Dovedale Primary School many times, along Dovedale Road, L18, in Allerton, just across from Penny Lane. (The school's entrance is actually on Herondale Road.) But I went to another Allerton primary school, Booker Avenue. Back then both schools were feeders for Quarry Bank School, the high school John attended between 1952 and 1957 and I between 1971 and 1976. John, his teachers concluded, was a bright lad "destined to fail."

He had an attitude problem, a chip on his shoulder, frequently fighting and smoking, playing truant and generally goofing about making trouble. He'd regularly talk back to teachers, get detention. When he and Quarry Bank chums Pete Shotton, Rod Davis, and Eric Griffiths formed the pre-Beatles band the Quarrymen (along with non-Quarry mates Len Garry and Colin Hanton), the new Headmaster William E. Pobjoy supported John's musical inclinations; if it kept him off the streets, and out of mischief, so be it, said Mr. Pobjoy. John failed his "O-Level" Art exam; but Mr. Pobjoy arranged an interview for him with Liverpool Arts College. Ordinarily, the College wouldn't let anybody in who failed O-Level Art. But they let John in; he talked his way in.

I say "Mr. Pobjoy" because that's what we used to call him. He was a progressive young head in his mid-thirties in John's day, early fifties in mine; but Quarry did nothing for me. No subject or teacher lit my fire there. I was "destined to fail," too, somehow wanted to fail. All I can remember doing on the run up to my O-Levels was playing poker dice in the school gardener's shed, sneaking off when I could, with other members of the "4 Aces" gambling club: Macker, Evo, Grimmo, and me; that's what we called ourselves, the 4 Aces. The others called me "Megs." All of us were losers even as we tried to win. None of us had a cent to our name. One time, I remember owing £26 ($40), a small fortune in those days. I had a bad losing streak at poker dice. It became my addiction, ensuring I failed most of my exams. A roll of the dice never abolished chance.

I lived in Garston, L19; John along Menlove Avenue, number 251, L18, the other side of Calderstones Park, closer to school than me, near to the Salvation Army children's home at Strawberry Fields, which was up Beaconsfield Road's steep hill. Menlove Avenue was always considered the posher side of town. John's was a bigger inter-war semi than ours. Garston was more run down; my mother and father weren't very educated, manual workers both. I didn't go to college after school, not until ten years after, after I'd taught myself—or rather learned other things. At one gig in 1957, the Quarrymen played in my backyard at Garston's Wilson Hall. Lennon & Co. hailed from Allerton and Woolton, more affluent suburbs, so would have appeared poncey rich kids to an audience of laborers and teddy boys, working class heroes. After the gig, neighborhood toughies chased the band, planning to beat them up. John and the others just about fought them off, legged it away, leaping onto a passing bus to safety.

The Beatles were never my band. I heard their music all the while, everywhere, throughout my childhood and adolescence; but I never really listened. They were just there, in the background. My aunt Emily, my mother's younger sister, listened to the Beatles all the time. She'd play "Michelle" over and over again, a scratched 45 rpm, on her old record player, in a bedroom she shared with my elder sister. "Michelle, ma belle...I love you, I love you, I love you, that's all I want to say..." My aunt Emily had a rather tragic life; "Michelle" comforted her somehow. I never knew it then. I could hear it playing through the downstairs ceiling. Emily came to live with us after her mother and father, my nan and grandad, died in quick succession, both of lung cancer, like my mother. My grandad was a coal man. They'd lived together in a little "terrace" house in Holden Street, central Liverpool, off Upper Parliament Street, in Toxteth, where my mother grew up. Heavy smokers all, it's one reason I've never smoked.

In the mid-1960s, they'd received a letter from the council telling them that their terrace house was condemned, that it was deemed a slum, and they would have to move out soon. The street and the surrounding neighborhood would be demolished, residents shipped out to a spanking new abode at Cantril Farm, beyond the city limits in Knowsley. It was a brave new prefabricated world, a mass housing project the likes of which Jane Jacobs had already condemned in *Death and Life of Great American Cities*. But authorities in Britain paid little attention to Jane, just as they paid little attention to homegrown critics. They'd not listened to British sociologists Peter Willmott and Michael Young who, in the late 1950s, had published *Family and Kinship in East London*. The pairing warned of how centralized bureaucratic housing programs were ignoring the needs of the people they intended to serve. Willmott and Young said Bethnal Green's slum clearance plan would devastate tight-knit class and kinship networks. The East London neighborhood, like Toxteth, was poor and crumbling, in dire need of attention. Yet it was also a world rich in social relations and mutual support systems—vital resources for healthy social and community life. *Family and Kinship in East London*, like *Death and Life of Great American Cities*, eventually had a huge influence on planners and policy-makers. In Liverpool, though, it all came too late (or too early).

Before long, Cantril Farm began to bear another label: "Cannibal Farm." Even before it was finished, the estate was falling apart. Tower blocks were leaky and damp; there was no soundproofing between apartments; communal corridors smelt of piss, lacked lighting, and what lighting there was often didn't work; elevators were usually broken. There was no public transport, no doctors' surgeries, no shops, no nothing, a high-rise wilderness set in a wilderness, a fallow field in a fallow field, cut-off from anywhere, from any memorable past and any discernible future. It was row upon row of austere breeze-block towers, homes for twenty thousand wounded denizens, mushrooming on land the council acquired at a snip. Little wonder my Nan didn't last very long in this wilderness, nor my grandad. Both died a few years later, broken hearts within a broken community.

Shortly after, my thirty-something aunt Emily developed ovarian cancer. Before she died, at forty—same age as ex-Beatle John—she came to live with us. For a few happy years she went into remission, quit her job at Woolworth's, managed to live on sickness benefit, and listened to "Michelle" a lot. Her single bed was shoved into the alcove of my sister's bedroom, tight against the far wall, near the airing cupboard, making room for my sister's own bed. Above her bed, my aunt Emily had scotch-taped a poster onto the wall, of Omar Sharif in *Dr. Zhivago*—after Boris Pasternak's novel and David Lean's film. My aunt Emily wasn't bothered about Boris Pasternak or Russian literature or director David Lean; it was Omar Sharif she idolized, along with the Beatles, two of her burning passions. I remember the poster's caption: "A LOVE CAUGHT IN THE FIRE OF REVOLUTION." Yuri Zhivago looked dreamily out into the distance, with Omar's dark glowing eyes as radiant as ever; resting on his shoulders was the very beautiful head of Lara, played by the very beautiful Julie Christie. The beautiful couple cheered up my aunt's less than beautiful life.

It was her favorite film. We'd seen it together at the Plaza cinema in Allerton—me, my aunt Emily, and my mother. I remember being sick in the intermission. I'd eaten too much ice cream. Aunt Emily always spoiled her only nephew, gave me anything I wanted, often more than I needed. The chocolate ice cream came back up near the marble goldfish pond they had at the Plaza in those days. Shimmering turquoise illuminated the whole foyer, sparkling water, rippling and reflecting off the cinema's ceiling and walls. I don't remember much of Yuri and Lara's doomed love affair, nor anything about Aunt Emily's doomed love affairs; unmarried, she was likely a lifelong virgin. Yet she was besotted by Omar, never tired of reminding people that she had an intimate connection to Dr. Zhivago. And she didn't just mean that poster on her bedside wall.

Down the road from our house were a half-dozen little stores—a post office, a greengrocer, and a baker, all no more of course. Back then the greengrocer was Tushingham's, John

Tushingham's store, whom we all knew at our house. In a funny quirk of fate, John was actually dad of Rita, and Rita Tushingham, you might remember, was the actress who played Lara and Yuri's illegitimate love child— simply "the girl" in the film. She was the niece that General Yevgraf Zhivago (Alec Guinness) was searching for. I don't think my aunt Emily ever met Rita, or even saw Rita; she'd have dearly loved to have bumped into her at the counter where dad worked the bacon slicer. I don't think anybody ever saw Rita around pop's store after she'd become famous. You can't really blame her, preferring Omar Sharif and his glittering ice palace wonderland to dreary old Garston, where there was nothing to do and the sun never shone. But that didn't matter to my aunt Emily. She was merely glad that Rita was somehow close by, reinforcing her bond with Yuri, and with Omar, and with those dark radiant eyes staring out across my sister's bedroom.

Our house was pretty crowded in those years. I had the tiniest of box-room bedrooms; from my bed I could almost reach out and touch both sidewalls. I don't remember doing any homework, never reading or studying anything. Not sure where I'd have done it anyway. There was no space, little inclination, nothing to motivate me, no point. My grandad, my father's father, also lived with us and that closed the walls in even more. He took up the entire front room of our ground-floor, meaning we did everything in the single back room; ate, watched TV, entertained, got under each other's feet. My grandad had his bed in his room, an armchair, a small black and white TV set, a little table where he took all his meals, alone. He only ever came out to use the bathroom or to take his afternoon stroll. He'd always shout out, telling my aunt Emily to turn her music down. He didn't like it playing too loud, had no sympathy for anybody, the dying included. Each morning, no matter what the weather, he donned his old worn tweed suit, with its waistcoat, plus a tie, had a cooked breakfast prepared by my mother, at nine o'clock prompt, fried bread, bacon, tomatoes, and an egg, a "Jim Special" we called it. His name was James—"Lord Jim," we anointed him.

By contrast, he always called me "Charlie"; not sure he ever remembered my name, or wanted to. He never bought an Xmas or birthday present, never bought me anything. He behaved like an aristocrat in exile, an aristocrat retired from reading the meter for the Gas Board. At one o'clock, without fail, he'd expect lunch served, again by my poor old ma, a "biscuit sandwich"—white sliced bread, cheese, Branson pickle, a digestive cookie, a cup of tea. For dessert, he only ever ate tinned fruit, mandarins or pears in syrup, never anything fresh. At six o'clock, he'd call out for "tea," after which he'd settle back into a night's TV. So it went, with tyrannical regularity. One day, during a summer heatwave, dressed in full suit, all buttoned up, he sat in a deckchair in the garden, fell asleep in the shade, and died. My mother found him dribbling at the mouth. My sister and I both cheered.

Every time I've heard "Michelle" since, I feel sad. Those Beatles' records don't have positive associations in my life. That's probably why I used to shudder outside the Dakota, thinking of John and the Beatles, glad I was in New York not Liverpool, no longer throwing up at the Allerton Plaza; poor John; poor Aunt Emily; poor me at Quarry Bank. As I grew up, I knew I needed something more than the Beatles, needed a different sort of music, not one that took me back to Liverpool, that made me sentimental, mawkish, but one which propelled me forward. *Something Else!* was Ornette Coleman's debut jazz album from 1958, which set the tone (and tonality) for me. Besides, there was nothing about my Liverpool past to feel sentimental about, other than that world is long dead, no more, people largely forgotten, some best forgotten. My aunt Emily, my mother, my nan and grandad, Holden Street, the old Liverpool I knew, the 4 Aces, Lord Jim, Tushingham's, Dr. Zhivago staring out—all gone. Quarry Bank has even gone, changing its name years back. My old playground is a supermarket, the Smithdown Road hospital where I was born an Asda (owned by Walmart). Even Cantril Farm has gone, not-so-solid breeze-block melted into air, along with all those high hopes.

The day Marshall melted into air I was far from the Dakota and Central Park, far from the Upper West Side. They, too, had become distant memories, those strolls in the park, by the park, down Central Park West. They'd become dreamlike, even New York became dreamlike, may never have really happened. Had I imagined it all? It felt like it some days. I was riding around Cambridge, England, on my bike, doing some afternoon shopping. I checked my email on my phone; David Harvey was in my inbox; typically terse, he wrote: "Marshall died this morning." It read like a line from Camus, from the opening of *The Stranger*. Meursault was indifferent to his mother's dying; I broke down when I heard of Marshall's, started sobbing uncontrollably, embarrassed that I was in the street, walking my bike.

It was a devastating line: *Marshall died this morning*. And the date—September 11, I mean, 9/11—how could it be? Another tragic New York day, another tragic New York death? How did it happen? David hadn't said. Suicide? I couldn't believe that; Marshall? Never. "I chose life," Marshall had once told me, reluctantly talking about the death of his son Marc. "I could have given up then," he said. "But I wanted to live." I can hear him saying that now: *I wanted to live*. And now he was dead and so was my New York. But perhaps it had already died long ago.

I remembered Marshall writing about 9/11, days after it occurred. “The sense of loss thickens the city air,” he wrote, “like the murky smells that drift uptown, merge with the incense from the candles on the streets, and make it suddenly hard to breathe. Then the smell is gone; then it comes back. ‘Does it hurt?’ ‘Only when I breathe.’” Everything changed after 9/11. America changed, New York changed for me, changed the way I saw it. It didn’t change for the better. Around this time I’d applied for a job, at the New School, a job I thought might have my name on it; a lot of others thought the same, that I was a good fit, and it a good fit for me. It would get me out of my sink hole in Massachusetts, consolidate my New York, give me something I’d hitherto not been able to get: *a New York job*. I could even dump the car, let the pound take it away, forever!

There were plenty of temporary gigs going for academics, adjunct gigs, gigs where big institutions didn’t have to pay much. Hey, it’s New York, you’ll work for nothing just to be here! They seemed to believe this, those big institutions. I didn’t. I was ambivalent about being an academic anyway. Maybe being a tenured one in New York might help me get over it? I had published a couple of books that year, was writing in *The Nation*, kept myself busy, was enthusiastic about stuff I’m no longer enthusiastic about. I was ready and able. So the presentation. So the interview.

So I didn't get the job. They gave it someone else, less suited yet more business-like, more bullshitting. I wasn't liked. Arrogance? Bad reputation? I never knew. Perhaps they sensed my ambivalence, my agnosticism?

It was a big blow for Corinna and me. Our hopes of moving up in the New York world were dashed: getting a bigger apartment, settling down for old age, having a family. Our New York friends said there were always other jobs. But it occurred to me there might not be any jobs for my type. I didn't feel like waiting around. I was hurt and every time I get hurt I feel the need to take it out on someone, to lash out, even if that someone were a city. I'd been imagining myself like Marshall, a scholar like him. But that was another generation, another era. And then 9/11. And then we decided we needed to get away, go someplace where we could take a bath. (When people politely speak of a "water-closet," that's literally what we had at our place.) We treated ourselves, at great expense, to a few nights at the American Hotel in Sag Harbor, around the corner from where Spalding Gray lived. I never saw Spuddie anywhere around town that weekend. I was on the lookout. Ground Zero had stopped smoldering. Yet America's political landscape was on fire, being burned to the ground.

Springtime arrived after a long winter. Sitting on a low wall, close to Harbor Books, I basked in regenerating sunshine, thinking how great it was to be in America, here, today, warming myself, photosynthesizing, happily watching the Saturday afternoon Hampton world go by. Corinna and I had a lovely walk on Sunday, began feeling optimistic again after months of gloom. We both took baths and later went to the hotel bar, drinking lots of white wine. We ate dinner. Then thought we'd check out Oscar night at the hotel's TV room, full of fat guys, neatly dressed in Ralph Lauren and loafers, smelling like they'd just been puffing on cigars outside, reeking of money as well as tobacco.

Drinking for hours, we were in high spirits when Diane Lane opened the envelope to award the Academy Award for Best Documentary to Michael Moore, for *Bowling for Columbine*. Diane seemed delighted. Michael clambered on stage, along with his wife and camera crew and the other nominees. He thanked everybody, laughed, cleared his throat, laughed again, and said jokingly, "I've invited my fellow documentary nominees on the stage with us because we like non-fiction. We like non-fiction and we live in fictitious times. We live in the time where we have fictitious election results that elect a fictitious President. We live in a time where we have a man sending us to war for fictitious reasons. Whether it's the fiction of duct tape or the fiction of orange alerts, we are against this war, Mr. Bush. Shame on you, Mr. Bush, shame on you. And anytime you've got the Pope and the Dixie Chicks against you, your time is up!"

The Oscar audience began stirring, booing and cheering at the same time, though maybe the boos were winning out. Corinna and I were thrilled at Michael Moore's gall and guts, at his incredible courage and composure, dishing the dirt, the honest truth. He was right, needless to say. We both rose to our feet in the American Hotel and cheered loudly, clapped loudly, and shouted loudly: *"Yeah, go Michael Moore! Go Michael Moore! Go Michael Moore!"*

We went on cheering and clapping until…until...we realized we were alone, that it was only us who clapped and cheered, who were on our feet, who supported Michael Moore; everybody else went quiet, deathly and deadly quiet, unimpressed. They were all-American, supported their President, supported their country, didn't want anyone disturbing their Sunday TV or their all-American way of life. Truth or falsity never came into it. We got frosty looks afterward, especially when they heard we weren't American. The reactionary air thickened. We felt very Other. We'd always felt very Other no matter where we went. Yet tonight Corinna and I felt another kind of Otherness; somehow it was bidding us not goodnight but *farewell.* My allergy toward nationalism brought me out in hives. It was the beginning of the end of our American dream which only hours earlier had been rekindled under the sun. That radiant sunshine had been eclipsed by melancholy Saturn. And we were only two hours from the big city, not somewhere in Middle America, in hicksville. Now, it all felt like hicksville. (Hicksville, we laughed on the drive back to Manhattan, was a real place, even nearer to New York than Sag Harbor.)

That summer I walked away from my job in Massachusetts, sold my old jalopy to one of our doormen, gave it away really, for five-hundred dollars, and wondered what on earth I was going to do next—for work as well as for life. It was odd to now feel at odds with the city I loved, once loved, still love, now hated. Why had it soured me so? Why was I so reactive? Why did I take things so personally? Then Marshall told me of an opening at CCNY. He could help, he said, because he knew people up there. The Colin Powell Center was looking to expand its program. It'd be great to have you at CCNY, Marshall said. He made some calls, fixed up a meeting for me, was sweet and considerate. Boy, how he loved that institution, the City College of New York; it was the only job he ever had, begun in 1967, and he was still there, still at it, still as passionate about his teaching as ever. It had been a noble and Nobel establishment. Founded in 1847, high up in Hamilton Heights in Harlem, CCNY was the US's first free public educational institution, the "Harvard of the Proletariat," with its handsome Gothic architecture, more Ivy League than the Ivy League, producing ten Nobel laureates, many of whom hailing from modest local stock.

Marshall had landed in the right place and dedicated a good deal of his life to CCNY. He was one of the few academics I knew who was genuinely proud of the place they worked. So why was it that I felt so skeptical? Maybe it was the center itself? I mean, *Colin Powell* Center. I was grateful to Marshall and went up to speak to Vincent Boudreau, then the center's director, today CCNY's president. Yet the center gave me the creeps. Henry Kissinger and Madeleine Albright were on its advisory board. General Colin L. Powell graduated from CCNY in 1958, became a four-star general, a national security advisor and, more latterly, a Secretary of State—as impressive an alumni as you'd find anywhere. Now, his namesake center was involved in the social sciences, in international affairs and global governance, training future world leaders and cutting-edge scholars. I had a few problems with all this, perhaps for good reason: Powell peddled the case for military action against Saddam Hussein and the "weapons of mass destruction" he supposedly had, addressing a plenary session of the United Nations; all of which, as Michael Moore had said, were "fictitious reasons" for going to war. They were lies. Did Powell know it? Was he merely towing the line, closing rank and following orders?

They offered me a position that meant a pay cut, doing a job that any graduate student could do. It wasn't clear how I could sustain a life in Manhattan earning so little. I wasn't turned on, knew it wasn't right. Years back, I would have thought this a dream come true: CCNY, a colleague of Marshall's, wow! Now, it felt all wrong, something I just couldn't go through with. There was this thing inside me tugging away, pulling me back, telling me I'd lose my integrity there. It was an instinct. I wasn't that desperate. I preferred to do nothing than to work at the Colin Powell Center; but how to break this news to Marshall who thought CCNY was worth it at any cost?

The last time I spoke to Marshall was at Yom Kippur, on the phone, a week before we moved to Europe. Corinna had been offered a job in Geneva; her turn now. I would follow her as she'd followed me. We were going to live in France, just across the border, start a new life together, begin another chapter. I would write; Corinna would go to her office each day, to work on food, consolidate her career now that I had flunked mine. I let it flunk. I would figure something out, become a recluse or whatever, disappear, write about donkeys. I mean, life goes on, right? Marshall had forgiven me, was gentle on the other end of the line, enquiring, though remained perplexed. I was from the working class, he said, I had to work, had to labor to earn a living. I had no trust fund to live off. Did I really know what I was doing?

Only a few weeks prior he'd told me that at CCNY "*his reputation was mud.*" I had turned the job there down, let him down, made him look silly because he'd been telling everybody about me, excited about my coming. I felt bad, really bad. CCNY didn't give two hoots whether I came or not. I was surprised that Marshall's reputation there should be so fragile after more than thirty years of service. But that's what he said, "*my reputation was mud.*" I was very hurt that I had hurt him. It was the last thing I wanted to do in the whole world. Yet now, on the Jewish Day of Atonement, he was over it, wished me well, *shalom!*

Years later, his widow, Shellie, told me Marshall was sad I quit New York because he enjoyed hanging out with me. This cut me up when she said it. She told me in a Starbucks near Penn Station, her choice of venue. We hadn't seen each other for years. She'd been tippling vodka beforehand; she was so nervous meeting me again, she said; I was so nervous meeting her again, I said. She was on her way to Philadelphia to see her sister, taking the train. She needed the vodka for that, too, she'd said. We cried together over Marshall. He missed hanging out with me, that's all, she said, that's why he was so sad and angry I'd left.

One of my most enduring images of Marshall is seeing him at the Lincoln Plaza cinema. Often, on a Saturday night, the four of us would take in a movie. We'd meet up at his place on West End and take the 1 train together from 103rd Street and Broadway, his local stop, down to Lincoln Center at 66th Street. Then we'd walk down a few blocks to the cinema. Getting to and from the subway, and venturing up and down its steps, was always slow going for Marshall. By the time we got to the cinema there weren't many tickets left. I can still see Marshall now, his great bulk only adding to the momentum, like a downhill skier, frantically hobbling down the aisle, grabbing those last remaining seats, invariably in the front row, almost *under* the screen. We were so close we had to tilt our heads backward. We could see the resolution of the film, like a giant Seurat canvas, tiny juxtaposed multicolored dots shifting before us. Anybody who didn't think Marshall could move fast was wrong. I'd seen it with my own eyes, his Olympian speed-hobble. It only added to the delight, to my memories. Those Saturday nights out were Saturday nights out with Marshall. It had nothing to do with cinema. I'd have done anything, gone anywhere, just to be with him.

Knee problems plagued him for years. A few years before he died he'd had surgery for knee replacement, which, "if it works," he'd said, "will help me walk tall for a while," help him fight against old age— quixotically, he'd said. He never did really walk tall afterward, nor get the chance to age quixotically. I'll always remember him hobbling, and stooping, a damaged shuffler, an earthy Sancho Panza rather than any knightly Don Quixote.

I just couldn't sustain the intensity he had for New York, bear the weight of all those contradictions, couldn't do it like him. I thought I could, could devote myself to New York. But when I was forced to confront it, and confront myself, I knew its high price wasn't worth it. The negatives started to invade my head-space as well as my living space. I had to leave to find my own way, to do my own thing, to be myself, not something else, some-one else. There were too many someone elses around me. The New York I'd been living in beforehand was an imaginary New York. I'd first seen it in 1970, but ever since I imagined it through books and film. It became a city that I appropriated when I read and watched.

I knew it from the Beats, from *Pull My Daisy*, from Spalding Gray and Woody Allen, from Andre Gregory and Wally Shawn, from Grace Paley and Jane Jacobs, from diners full of poets where I. B. Singer encountered working men and women, ordi-nary folk, Ray Carver's folk. They all hung out together, could afford to. It was the New York of artists and rebels, people who came, and stayed, because they preferred to be poor, preferred to struggle in the city rather than be better off elsewhere. Yet when I arrived in person, to live, when the accidents of my life brought me there, little, if anything, remained of this world. Its traces were so faint that there was no path to lead me from this past into a prospective future. There was no continuity between the then and the now. I was trapped somewhere in between, feeling unwanted and unnecessary, my imaginary world no more.

It was Marshall's New York I'd always wanted to inhabit, which might have been a New York existing only in Marshall's head; not a real New York, not on any grid plan, but a normative one, a New York that should be, ought to be, could be. My New York operated on the same ontological plane as Marshall's. I wanted it to. It was in another state of Being and Becoming. I wanted to speak in his register, affirm the same structure of feeling as his, mix the city with literature, literature with the city, anoint them both with pure unadulterated love. Whenever Marshall talked about cities, he was really talking about literature, about books. Wherever he talked about literature, about books, he was really talking about cities.

Somebody who got this as much as anybody was John Leonard, Marshall's old pal who passed away in 2008. Onetime literary editor at *The New York Times* and *The Nation*, Leonard commissioned many reviews from Marshall for the latter magazine throughout the 1980s and 1990s. Reviewing *All That Is Solid Melts into Air* in the *Times*, in 1982, Leonard said: "I've read Goethe, Marx, Baudelaire, and Dostoevsky. I've been to Leningrad. Berman has been somewhere else." His work of nonfiction, Leonard said, "is secretly a novel. I love this book and wished I believed it."

There was the terrible realization that somewhere, somehow, over the years, my love affair with New York had died. We had grown apart, become too familiar with each other, started to argue, lie, and cheat on one another. Its reality began crushing my imagination, cramping my style. My wish-image had to learn how to pay the monthly maintenance, to become a winner while remaining a loser. I didn't want to become a rich slave. My writing had no stock value. And those characters I associated with New York, characters I dearly loved, the places I once knew, ate and drank coffee in, the used bookstores I'd frequent—almost all of it had gone, had died, was dead was dead, as Kerouac once said. Now Marshall had gone, was dead. I felt like I was living out *Howl*, embodying Ginsberg's raving lament: "Dreams! adorations! illuminations! the whole boatload of sensitive bullshit!... Visions! omens! hallucinations! miracles! ecstasies! gone down the American river!" Or maybe, more prosaically, it was simply how Joan Didion had put it: *"Goodbye to all that."*

Cities are two-faced. They're objective and subjective realities, objective and subjective at the same time. The objective city is the hard city, made of bricks and mortar, physical and structural, a physicality people have to deal with, the prison-house of past actions, embodied in an object—a building or a space. Sometimes these objects and spaces overwhelm us, makes us feel small, are the walls that prop up our lives yet somehow also hem us in. Subjectivity gives meaning to this objective reality, tries to deal with it, to humanize it, to re-appropriate it through active consciousness, through living being. The subjective city is the soft city, the city of the mind, of human consciousness, of human frailty and ambiguity. The link between objective and subjective realms is a constant battle, an inexorable dialectic. I'm not sure there will ever be any reconciliation.

I remember some days in Manhattan yearning for a bit of mystery, for something more secret and subjective, a hidden history. Everything was so out in the open, so obvious, those streets and avenues, all clearly marked out, all following a rational grid plan, an objectivity. Of course, this was the openness I loved, its physical vitality, that freed itself of repression, that howled in the street. Yet there were times when, strangely, I wanted things to be more repressed, more reserved, more out of sight, more cerebral, quieter and unspoken. Life was directly in your face, sheer objectivity. I began dreaming of a secret, hidden calmness, a rabbit hole, someplace where you could cut out the noise, find warm, cozy subjectivity.

One of the great books about urban subjectivity is *Invisible Cities.* In it, the Italian novelist Italo Calvino sets up an imaginary dialogue between the Kublai Khan, the powerful Tartar emperor, and the intrepid explorer Marco Polo. Reclining on luscious cushions, they converse in a dazzlingly opulent garden in Khan's palace. Polo has journeyed to the outer reaches of Khan's vast empire. Now he recounts to Khan tales of his urban adventures. Khan has often dreamt of those exotic cities that are his own; he's never actually seen them, never been there, but has envisioned them, almost anticipated all that Polo tells him. Somehow Khan has strolled around those cities already, in his mind. "The descriptions of cities Marco Polo visited had this virtue: you could wander through them in thought, become lost, stop and enjoy the cool air, or run off."

Do my dreams correspond to reality? Khan asks Polo. The explorer says they do. But we can't be sure he's telling the truth. Perhaps he's only recalling his own fantasies, because he's describing cities that don't appear on any map. They're real yet fantastical places, composite yearnings. After a while, we realize that Khan and Polo mightn't be talking about cities at all—at least none we recognize in bricks and mortar, in glass and steel. They're ideas, really, thought experiments: "You take delight," the wise emperor says, "not in a city's seven or seventy wonders but in the answer it gives to a question." Later on, Polo muses on his explorations, wondering if all along he's only been trying to conceive the perfect city in his head, piecing it together, bit by bit, fragment by fragment, forming a totality made of instances separated in time and space. At the end of their dialogue, he confesses to Khan: "If I tell you that the city toward which my journey tends is discontinuous in space and time, now scattered, now more condensed, you must not believe the search for it can stop."

So the journey, whatever that journey might be, can never really stop. Since leaving New York, I've been wandering, never finding my place, never stopping in one place too long to find it. I was no longer taking delight in "seven or seventy wonders" but in the answers these staging posts gave to my questions. I wasn't alone. I've been wandering with Corinna, and *we* have never really found our place, nor any real answers. We tried living in the countryside. We did find slow calmness, the warm, cozy subjectivity that I'd once yearned for, in an Alpine village, and then in a poor, exhausted mountainous region in a deserted Auvergne. For several years, we lived out a surreal French idyll, as far from Manhattan as you could possibly imagine. Only it was real.

But soon enough it became too real. With slowness and peace the rot set in. We needed stimulation again, contrast and contradiction. Things never worked out for Corinna in Geneva. Our life was turning into a desperate thought experiment. I began talking about cities in the imaginary, and most times I was talking to myself. Perhaps it was better that way. Perhaps it was like Marco Polo, who, remember, in the end comes clean with Kublai Khan: "Every time I describe a city," he said, "I am saying something about Venice." "What else do you believe I have been talking to you about?" "To distinguish the other cities' qualities," Polo said, "I must first speak of a city that remains implicit. For me that is Venice." For me, of course, that implicit city is New York. Her skyscrapers reach up to the heavens of my inner landscape.

We went to Brazil, with our young daughter, born in a little French town called Issoire. We all went to São Paulo for a year, for Corinna's work, to a dizzying metropolis, double New York's size. We'd recognized we needed speed again, a fast life, a noisy life, bizarre as it sounds. We needed the magic potion of being amongst people again, lots of people, of being out on busy streets. Our daughter needed to grow up in public, not in private. I'd hoped I could write a book that conjured up this spell-like potion, that somehow tapped it politically, captured São Paulo's intensity and pulse. Most days, I sat writing in Dom José Café in Jardim

Paulista, at the junction of ruas Artur de Azevedo and Oscar Freire, near hospital das clínicas. Whenever I lifted my head out of my text, I watched a vast metropolitan developing world go by. Everything was out in the open. Even the inside was open to the outside. There weren't any closed doors to cafés in Brazil, nor closed windows, nothing physical to prevent the inner space spilling out into the outer space—and vice versa. Café chairs and tables entered the street; the street became part of the café's popular stage. There was a porosity between private solace and communal culture. The private self had no four walls to render itself invisible. It was nothing like New York, nothing northern or Anglo-Saxon: in São Paulo, peace and noise, day and night, outer light and inner darkness, street and home, all interpenetrated.

Outside, a ceaseless flow of people, a phantasmagoria of colors; cars crawled by, honking horns in the jam; motorcycles rattled by. The din was outside and inside, inside the café; never did it seem to bother. Then, a weird thing happened. Late afternoon, for a half hour, the heavens opened, a Biblical downpour drenched everything and everyone. Flooded streets became gushing rapids, flushing away debris. Suddenly, overhead traffic lights went down. And, at this point, things became weird: instead of chaos, instead of incident and accident, instead of even more honking horns and erratic traffic, all went eerily quiet. Calmness prevailed. Motorists and motorbikes, aware of apparent danger, stopped beeping, drove cautiously, responsibly, attentive and tentative at every crossroad. It was like watching some beautiful synchronized ballet, vehicles, with the sound turned down. No sooner had the red lights started flashing again than the racket recommenced.

I tried to write about São Paulo but couldn't. I felt no intimacy toward the city, didn't fall in love with it. Perhaps not getting too het up about it helped me live in it, enjoy it... I kept things Platonic. I'd hoped to find in it the crazy Latin American romance I'd imbibed within the pages of Gabriel García Márquez's *One Hundred Years of Solitude*. I remembered seeing a photo of the Colombian Márquez, wearing an open-necked denim shirt, looking robust and workerist, pinned above Marshall's work station, inspiring Marshall's own romance, his love in a time of urbanism. I'd been blown away when I'd read *One Hundred Years of Solitude* because it convinced me that reality could be represented differently, that more acute and astute forms of subjectivity could create a more advanced sense of realism, a different type of objectivity.

The bizarre shenanigans of the Buendía family in the town of Macondo, hacked out of the middle of damp Colombian jungle, was a saga of a paradise found and lost, a mad dream of damaged characters whose only goal in life was to live out a magnificent human adventure. "Things have a life of their own," Melquíades, the gypsy magician reminded José Arcadio Buendía. "It's simply a matter of waking up their souls." José Arcadio hardly needed reminding: Macondo's patriarch's "unbridled imagination always went beyond the genius of nature and even beyond miracles and magic." He taught his two wayward sons, José Arcadio and Aureliano, the wild man who'd eventually run off with the gypsies, and the withdrawn child who'd become one of the nation's most fabled radicals, to read and write; "and he spoke to them about the magical wonders of the world, not only where his learning had extended, but forcing the limits of his imagination to extremes."

And yet, before long, I recognized that magical wonders didn't exist in the objective reality of São Paulo, with its gridlocked streets, crumbling infrastructure and grinding poverty. The only wonderment I could find was subjectively mustered up inside my own head, in my occasional mad leaps of the imagination. It wasn't so much idealism as really making the mind work, making it come to life, putting it into thought-practice. Out of it came a purely make-believe book, *Magical Marxism*, about nowhere in particular, nobody in particular, which Marshall blurbed. It hadn't been my idea to contact him. But he wrote words I cherish, making the book sound better than it is. When the book was done, I got to wonder whether being in a city, in a very big city, had helped this magic flow? Maybe the magic was incubated in this giant magician's melting pot? Maybe its vaporous spell wafted over me sat in Dom José Café?

My mind wanderings continued in Mexico City. I remember looking down on the city, in awe, shimmering in glorious sunshine, from thirty-six floors up in the sky, from a plush building in Polanco. The green expanse of Chapultepec was before me, sliced apart by Paseo de la Reforma, itself crisscrossed by an enormous multi-tiered expressway—Circuito Interior—in the distance, gridlocked with traffic. The city seemed to end only at the horizon, at the foothills of faraway mountains. At times, Mexico City seemed to stretch beyond the horizon, beyond anything as-yet recognizable, as if it were already staking out some new interstellar planetary urban turf.

At street level, I wandered through passageways named after Ancient philosophers and famous scribes; Alejandro Dumas led me into Parque Lincoln, a verdant little oasis with its scrubbed white clock tower and statue of Abraham, the park's namesake. I strolled along empty paths. I smelt a bookstore somewhere, thought of Walter Benjamin, that intrepid urbanist and bookwormer, and understood what he meant when unpacking his library: each book on the shelf, he'd said, was like a little memento of a time spent wandering the city streets, a tiny brick with which you could reconstruct past urban environments and imagine new ones to come. "How many cities," he said, "have revealed themselves to me in the marches I undertook in the pursuit of books!"

Then I found one. Or maybe it found me: Cafebrería El Péndulo, a bookstore-cum-café, with an inner atrium of immense beauty. Light flooded in. Exotic vegetation invaded the stacks. Everywhere titles were delicately encased in cellophane. Suddenly I saw one I had to have. I prised it open, liberated it. Daubed across its front cover, in uppercase, was: THE SAVAGE DETECTIVES, by Roberto Bolaño. A Santiago native, Bolaño grew up in Mexico City, studied law yet dropped out, yearned to be a writer, and, in the 1970s, helped establish a group of combustible wayward poets. They heckled and hassled and threw ripe tomatoes at literary conventionality, lusting for literature in life. In *The Savage Detectives* they called themselves "Visceral Realists."

The book's heroes are anti-heroes: Ulises Lima and Arturo Belano, a poetic duo, Underground Men who haunt the city's grungy bars and cafés, like Café Quito along Calle Bucareli—real life Café La Habana with its checkered beige and white flooring. Ulises and Arturo are poor and young yet already men of the world, haunted by grown-up demons. They talk about Comte de Lautréamont as if he were their best pal. They're on the trail of another phantom, Visceral Realism's mythical poet Godmother, Cesárea Tinajero, who, in the 1920s, disappeared into the lost sands of the Sonora desert. Lima walks everywhere, never takes the bus or subway. Every book in the world for him is waiting to be read. He reads in his sleep, reads in the shower. Belano, meanwhile, carries in his back pocket folded photocopies of Raymond Queneau's verse, paper so crumpled it looks more like origami, "a startled paper flower with its petals splayed towards the four points of the compass."

I read *The Savage Detectives* in a couple of sittings—or really in a couple of lyings—on my bed, propped up by a pillow, intermittently staring out the window into the sky, looking at the twinkling galaxy of lights below, liquid red and yellow flows, oscillating in some still-undiscovered nebula. I was looking at Mexico City while reading about Mexico City. I was there, physically present, in real Mexico City, in this great seething, sprawling metropolis yet was inside Bolaño's great seething, sprawling metropolis, too, inside his thought-landscape where places and words congeal, difficult to tell apart.

One character, Quim Font, was about my age, once a successful architect in La Condesa. But we quickly get wind of Quim's downward drift. His psychological disposition is troubled. He's moody and melancholic and often babbles bizarrely. Later, we hear he's been certified. He reflects on the books he's read over the years, read when happy, when sad, when thirsty for knowledge, when desperate for knowledge. You can't live your whole life in desperation, Quim says. That was Ulises and Arturo's big mistake. The passage from adolescence to adulthood, Quim says, is one from desperation to serenity, a regenerative process, learning how to embrace Proust and Thomas Mann's *The Magic Mountain*. A literature of desperation is "a literature of resentment," "full of sharp instruments and lynched messiahs"; it "doesn't pierce the heart the way a calm page, a carefully thought-out page, a technically perfect page does." "Seek oneself," Quim says, "lose oneself in strange lands. But with a guiding line."

I need to pin this message up near *my* work station, near my inspiration, my picture of Marshall, with his open arms, smiling in a radiant white suit, with a red shirt and bright yellow and brown tie; the tie might even be a Marc Chagall print, I can't quite tell. He looks like a cross between a Lower East Side rabbi and a stand-up comic, a bearded Lenny Bruce. When I see him here, happy, I feel sad, burdened by my sense of regret, some days as troubled as Quim. Quim's old neighborhood was La Condesa, my favorite part of Mexico City. I used to go there on foot, across Chapultepec, navigating some scary traffic arteries. I'd pass over the Circuito Interior on a rusty footbridge, into Condesa's dusty backstreets. Pavement cafés and trendy boutiques have just enough bohemian grunge to ward off bourgeoisdom. There are stunning buildings, like the Centro Cultural Bella Época, an Art Deco jewel, with Latin America's biggest bookstore, even bigger and more exotic than Cafebrería El Péndulo; thirty-five thousand titles shelter under a twenty-two thousand square-foot glass ceiling, looking like it was transplanted from Amazonia. You can relax on big leather sofas, read amid wild vegetation and floods of luminous white light.

There's another bookstore not far away, used, one Walter Benjamin would be proud of, Under the Volcano Books, a literary haven for anglophones on Calle Celaya. From the outside it looks like somebody's house, colonial-style, with blue arched iron grilling over its windows. You enter through an ornate archway into a darkened hall; Gauginesque artwork adorns the wall. A staircase leads you up to one small room, lined floor-to-ceiling with books. A young American mans the till. The bookstore calls itself "an embassy for the soul of the English-speaking world—its literature in Mexico...a web-free, Kindle-less island of analog time in a digital sea; a community center for Commonwealth and American expatriates in the most exciting, vibrant and accessible city on earth." I can't argue. I browse the Bolaño section, tell the young American I've read *The Savage Detectives*. He says check out Bolaño's poetry; Bolaño saw himself as a poet, a better poet than novelist. Look at *The Romantic Dogs*, the young American says. "I'm here with the romantic dogs / and here I'm going to stay." Bolaño said he wrote poetry in "the land of idiots." He scribbled outpourings in the "silent wing of the Unknown University."

The Savage Detectives' epigraph is by Malcolm Lowry, from *Under the Volcano* (1947), inspiration for the bookstore: "'Do you want Mexico to be saved? Do you want Christ to be our king?' 'No.'" *Under the Volcano* has another anti-hero, the so-called Consul, Lowry's doomed alcoholic alter-ego, the defrocked English civil servant in Mexico, Geoffrey Firmin. I tell the young American that Lowry hailed from Liverpool, like me—well, actually he hailed from New Brighton, across the River Mersey, close to Liverpool. Lowry was a rich kid, son of a wealthy cotton merchant, in the days when New Brighton was richer. I went to New Brighton for my childhood summer vacations, when it was poorer, taking the ferry across the Mersey, to Liverpool's Coney Island. Lowry was searching for something but somewhere along the way lost his guiding line.

Like the Consul, Ulises and Arturo drink mezcal. They, too, build their house under a volcano. They crop up everywhere, all over the world, have adventures galore, do every odd job under the sun, participate in Liberian civil wars and Nicaraguan revolutions. We don't hear anything more about their writings; they seem to have given up the act of writing as such. Their poetic blush is now living, inscribed in practical verse, viscerally real. Theirs is "the riddle of the poet who is lost yet survives." The truth is, "I don't remember anymore, but don't worry, the poet doesn't die, he loses everything, but he doesn't die."

Ulises shows up twenty years later, still apparently youthful but now in his forties, prowling Mexico City's Parque Hundido, a shadowy poet fugitive who has an affecting rendezvous, a make-believe encounter, with old man Octavio Paz, by then a Nobel laureate. Paz is accompanied by his housekeeper who recounts the clandestine event. Lima and Paz shake hands, sit down on a park bench. "How long did they talk? Not long. And yet from where I was sitting it was clear that it was a leisurely, calm, polite conversation." They spoke of Cesárea Tinajero. Years earlier, Ulises and Arturo had finally tracked her down, in the border town of Santa Teresa. She'd lived on her own for years in a little adobe house, in the middle of nowhere, a tragic woman who still radiated "immense humanity." One day, protecting Ulises and Arturo, she took a bullet in the chest. They buried her and afterward discovered her valedictory poem, the only poem Tinajero ever wrote.

Amazingly, it was just a few rows of lines, lines not words—wordless, made up of straight, wavy and jagged pen movements, zigzags resembling life's elemental path, verses of ups and downs and powerful feelings. What did the straight line mean? The horizon, calmness, still seas? And the wavy one? Hills on the horizon, movement, change? And the jagged? Shark's teeth, mountains on the horizon, choppy seas tossed by a gale? The poem said it all, the story of our life. It was also where *The Savage Detectives* trailed off. We're none the wiser about what happened to its stars, whether they lived or died. Is it true poets never die? We watch the detectives even while we're kept guessing, never quite knowing what they were investigating. "What's the mystery?" somebody asked. "Then the boys looked at me and said: 'there is no mystery.'"

A few years back, I received an invitation from an American university. They asked me to come and talk about "Europe." Europe? I mean, it was in chaos. Britain had just pulled the plug on it. The union was crumbling apart in disunity. What to say? At first, I wasn't sure I could say anything. But then I thought maybe I'd accept anyway, accept the challenge. Maybe thinking about this problem might help me think through my own identity. So I went and told the American audience I've never *felt* like a European, had no cause ever to see myself as a European. Up till now, "Europe" had figured only on my British passport, on my "official" identity papers. It said I belonged to the "European Union," that I was a "United Kingdom" citizen. But all those labels sounded existentially meaningless. I'd once held an American Green Card with this British passport, yet gave this Green Card up in France, at the American consulate in Lyon. Later, when I lived in Brazil, I paid my taxes in France, where I kept a house, at the same time as I had a Brazilian visa in my British passport. Things got muddled when I thought about my identity. I'm glad they're muddled. A lot of people I know have similar muddled identities, a lot more muddled than mine.

I felt like a hybrid person. I've been affected by many life (and death) experiences, both real and imagined, many cultures, many things I've read, places I've lived in, people I've encountered, characters in books I've embraced and befriended. I couldn't possibly reduce any of this to an abstract singular category, couldn't possibly identify with a nation, let alone a continent, and certainly nothing official or institutional. When I lived in America, I felt out of place. I felt out of place in France, too, in Europe, never felt French, never wanted to, was never allowed to; nor did my daughter, who was born there. When in France, I knew I'd been touched by America, by New York, still had it in my head somewhere, in my body—perhaps, even, in my soul. I don't know. Though in France I was never an Englishman despite being seen as an Englishman. Then I returned to Britain. And yet, there, here, it's impossible for me to think of myself as British, as English.

If anything, I want to live out the great proclamation of Baudelaire. I want to be what he called "a spiritual citizen of the universe." I want to be someone who finds a home everywhere, who feels they have *the right to belong everywhere.* I want to think of my identity as part of a much bigger reality, with a vaster horizon, to affirm this vast horizon, to not be afraid of its immensity as my home address. Baudelaire was fiercely loyal to Paris, his great muse. But his Paris was an environment that let the poet internalize the world. The world inhabited the city. It was where you could become a global citizen, a citizen of the world as well as an urban dweller—an urban citizen. It's maybe the greatest accolade one could think of for the city, for affirming its importance: a space that's open to the world.

There's something Ancient Greek about it. It seems that by identifying with a city, rather than a nation, you're on a safer democratic footing. There were no nation-states in Ancient Greece. Identity centered around the city—the city-state—around Athens. Athens's "first citizen" was Pericles. In his famous Funeral Oration, recounted by Thucydides in *History of the Peloponnesian War*,

Pericles commemorated the Athenian war dead. But he wanted citizens to remember how their system of city government had "a different attitude." It was based on openness not closure, discussion not denial. "Our city is open to the world," Pericles said, and Athenians should have "a confidence of liberality." "We have no periodical deportations," he continued. "The greatness of our city brings it about that all good things from all over the world flow into us." Athens was a paragon of urban citizenship everywhere, "a city that's the school of all Greece."

The city is a school. It teaches us things about how to live together, how to love together. For that reason, if ever I were to think of my own identity, think about how I might define it, I guess I'm *just a guy from Liverpool*. I'm neither English nor British, European nor American: just a guy from Liverpool, always will be. I would feel better if identity took on an urban characterization, Ancient Greek-style, if it were defined by which city you belong to; and belonging is always portable and transferable, adoptable and exchangeable. Layers get built into identity, thicken it, like a time-space palimpsest. I can take this identity with me anywhere I go, and it gets transported and translated. Liverpool has affected me permanently; I carry it with me wherever I am. I guess I'm a Liverpudlian spiritual citizen of the universe, shaped by living in New York. The most cosmopolitan New Yorkers might feel the same sense of open loyalty to their city in America; Marshall did. I tried.

Coming from Liverpool is my strange badge of honor worn *inside* my lapel, tucked away. There's no flag for this identity, no passport. Not a standard passport anyway. Proof of identity comes through a *shadow passport*, made out inside you, a phantom document stalking your official document. Something immutable is going on, a residue of something, a remainder, shaping you. What does it mean to talk about a Liverpool identity? Is its shadow passport stamped at the Pier Head with an image of the Liver Bird?

I've listened to those Lennon interviews. I know I have a similar chip on my shoulder emanating from somewhere, a shy kind of arrogance, a sense of humor—sometimes a black sense of humor. To come from Liverpool means frequently to self-dramatize, to act on impulse rather than reason, acting in full knowledge that it's not going to do you any good. Yet it's the right thing to do, the decent thing to do. An inbuilt sense of decency? Perhaps. A sense of sympathy with the downtrodden, a city that's historically accepted the downtrodden, been downtrodden itself? Maybe. Liverpool isn't "the North," isn't another grim northern British town. It *is* grim, of course, grimmer than grim sometimes. But the city draws its buoyant spirit from elsewhere, from the west, from Celtic Ireland, from across the Atlantic. It has kissed the

Blarney Stone, is hedonistic and sentimental, spends its money, drinks and parties, doesn't save, doesn't accumulate money, gives it away, dresses up, comes out at night, doesn't care about next morning. It's a city of the here and now, with a people of the here and now. It's a city that fights, has fought.

Back in the Eighties, during my twenties, Liverpool fought Margaret Thatcher's central government, her Conservative nation-state. It was a time when my own learning experience flourished. I'd been accepted at college—at Liverpool Polytechnic, a kind of CCNY institution that let in people like me, "mature" students without formal qualifications. Yet when I began, I quickly discovered Thatcher's government was taking apart the public sector that enabled me to go there for free. Liverpool was as anti-Thatcher as could be. In those days, a radical faction of the Labour Party called "Militant" controlled the city council, a Trotskyist "party within a Party." (It was virulently opposed to the party's own right-drifting leadership, too, under Neil Kinnock.) By the mid-1980s, the entire public sector in Liverpool seemed to be on strike. That's how I remember it anyhow. The Polytechnic entrance along Tithebarn Street, in the center of Liverpool, was blockaded, classes cancelled. I didn't know it then but I was getting an offsite extra-curricular education, learning urban theory and politics in the field, on the street. It was as if the city really were a school.

Chaotic days, chaotic weeks. Lockdown Liverpool. Militant engaged in the most real realism, call it visceral realism. They emphasized how the "capitalist" system couldn't deliver the goods—couldn't deliver housing for the needy, feed everyone, provide meaningful work—without being thrown into turmoil. So they deliberately threw it into turmoil. They built homes, not high-rises, loads of houses, thousands of them, all over the city, costing a lot, more money than the council had or would ever receive from Thatcher's central government. Hence the battle, a budget battle that became a class war: local versus national government, city versus nation-state, Liverpool versus the bourgeoisie.

I was supposed to be studying; instead, I wandered outside the college gates, around central Liverpool, my head astir with ideas. Everything about cities, their built environment, their control and management, their poverty and oppression, could be understood in terms of movements of capital investment, by variations in land rents and housing markets, by conflict between different social groups and classes, by the imposition of bureaucratic and rational structures and strictures. It was a fascinating picture unfolding around me, perplexing, personally and politically challenging. I remember my reverie getting interrupted by *noise*, by people. I was greeted by a vociferous mob. Thousands of people assembled under Liverpool's Town Hall balcony, carrying banners. Above, Militant councilors with megaphones.

They stood, defiant, on the balcony, bawling down, denouncing central government. *Maggie! Maggie! Maggie! Out! Out! Out!* They made rallying speeches. Below were supporters, below were enemies, cheering and jeering. I was there but somehow not there, elsewhere, torn between private impulses and political allegiances, between my innermost needs and my radical hopes. Maybe I'd remembered walking, years and years earlier, in another life, as a little boy, seizing my mother's hand, wanting protection, crossing over Exchange Flags, at the back of the Town Hall, on the way to the eye hospital. I'd no inkling then of what lay ahead, for me or for my mother. But I was alive and soon she wouldn't be. And now, years on, I was immersed in real life, unfurling on the streets, around me, in uncompromising form, a highly charged atmosphere that would affect me forever.

I got passionate like I never did at school. I was discovering a political and artistic underground, as well as a whole new mode of learning, a whole new mode of existence. I'd descended into a great wonderful rabbit hole, or perhaps into something darkly Dantesque, down circles of Liverpool's urban inferno, into the shady world of penniless literati, artists and writers, actors and wannabes, men and women of ideas. Some were authentic, some posturing, others untalented and on the dole. All hung out in grimy pubs, bars, and coffee shops where proletarian wisdom got produced. Marx, Machiavelli, Plato and Trotsky met Bill Shankly and the Fab Four. Dialogues were smart yet vulgar, intellectual yet loud, jokey yet heated—profane truths—as juices flowed and tempers flared. This was a new Liverpool I'd found, a wild life that sang in my veins; I was hoping it would never stop singing.

A Liverpool that dared to fight cropped up again not too long ago, in a peculiar way. Everybody knows Liverpool is a football-mad city, soccer crazy. The Beatles and Liverpool Football Club (F.C.) are its biggest exports. Maybe not everybody knows it has two major teams, Liverpool and Everton. (As a young lad, I supported Everton with my dad, the Blues rather than the Reds; we'd regularly go to Goodison Park to watch their ace championship winning team of the early Seventies.) But it's Liverpool F.C. that has dominated the city's soccer tradition. For many Liverpudlians, rather than a mere spectator sport, Liverpool F.C. is an entire way of life, literally what people live for, the air they breathe, the sea in which they swim. The title alone of David Peace's great doorstop of a novel, fictionalizing the life of Liverpool's legendary manager, Bill Shankly, captured these high stakes: *Red or Dead*. And here we're not talking about politics: this is all about about *jerseys*, about team colors. During the Sixties and early Seventies, Shankly, a Scot by birth, became a God in Liverpool, maybe even more than a God. Football was like socialism, he'd said. Admittedly, it wasn't about life and death: *football was more important than that*, Shankly said.

Thus, in a city besotted by soccer, it took a brave person to challenge it, to deny themselves it. Yet in the seventy-seventh minute of a match against Sunderland, in early 2016, over ten thousand fans got up and walked out. Anfield, home of Liverpool F.C., had witnessed its first organized mass walkout in its one hundred and thirty-two year history. The reason: a hike in the price of an already hiked match ticket, to £77 ($110). This was a protest against profit and monopoly, against a billion-dollar industry with TV advertising deals galore, and super-inflated players' wages and transfer costs—all of which were seemingly getting borne by ordinary working class Liverpudlians, hitherto loyal to their club. Soccer team owners know fans are unlikely to switch hometown allegiances. So they push and push, exploit and exploit.

The chickens were coming home to roost in the high-spending era of Tom Hicks and George Gillett, the American multi-millionaire duo who owned and mismanaged Liverpool F.C. between 2007-2010, leaving it financially-strapped and close to receivership. (Hicks was a former Dallas neighbor of George W. Bush, and bought from the latter the Texas Rangers basketball team in 1998.) Minutes before the mass exodus, fans in the Kop sang loudly, typically proudly: "ENOUGH IS ENOUGH, YOU GREEDY BASTARDS!" They did the right thing, the decent thing, even if it meant cutting their noses to spite their faces. Liverpool were winning 2-0 at that point. Sunderland scored two goals in the final thirteen minutes, drawing the game, and spooking club owners. Soccer isn't an elite game, fans proclaimed, not for VIPs, not like polo, not like golf, not for toffs. It's the people's sport, always will be. I've thought since then that if ever I were to write my Liverpool book, *The 77th Minute* would be its label. "It comes to us all, son," David Peace had Bill Shankly mouth. "And so you have to be prepared. You have to be ready, son. Because you have to decide how you will deal with it. Will it be with grace and with dignity? Or will it be with anger and with bitterness?"

Some of the last things Marshall ever wrote affirm this power of the city to overcome. It had been thrilling for me to hear he'd picked up the pieces of his old *Living for the City* book again, where we'd started out oh so long ago in that booth at the Metro Diner; only now Marshall was calling this book *The Romance of Public Space.* It had been thrilling to hear that we'd somehow ended up on common ground, too, seeing eye to eye about the city, finding unity after those years of disunity. When I'd met Shellie in Starbucks after that long absence, she'd let me read what Marshall had been writing the morning of his death. Shellie was trying to reassemble it all, get it published in a posthumous collection of essays, a final Bright Book of Marshall's Life and Times. He'd sketched out, in draft, a taster of what this book would entail:

"A very persistent psychological question in modern times is the question, *Who am I?* Erik Erikson, one of Freud's most creative followers, conceptualized this question as 'the problem of ego-identity.' He argued that everybody in the modern world finds their identity a problem in ways that are far more pressing and urgent than they used to be. In 1950, Erikson's masterpiece appeared, *Childhood and Society*, a hymn to the dream of America and the romance of the self. I got to know Erikson and his work fifteen years later, during the Vietnam War, fifty years ago. In the Cold War years, the great world powers nearly destroyed the world. Hope for a place where the self could feel at home still survived, but there were serious doubts that that place was a national state. The modern state was more dangerous than we had thought, its spiritual rewards less deep than we had hoped. Was there something else? Some other sort of place that could nourish people's sense of identity without crushing other people's identity? My idea in this book is to explore one of the most powerful ways in which this had happened through the ages. *That way is the city*. People can become themselves, can expand and enlarge themselves, through their connection with cities. They can find open and shareable forms of identity by *identifying with the city*."

One of Marshall's most striking essays, revised during the morning of September 11, 2013, was about the Bible, about the Garden of Eden, the "Bible's first public space." "Is God," Marshall wondered, "who has imagined the garden, constructed it, and pronounced it good, part of the public with Adam and Eve? Or does he see himself as the public, them as his temporary private guests?" God speaks of the forbidden fruit, and of the tree of knowledge of good and evil. If Adam and Eve eat from the tree, He will kill them. "The sun has hardly come up," Marshall said, "yet God seems to be looking for a fight." Adam and Eve are confronted with a dangerous message they must heed. This was how Marshall put it: "The lovely garden of Eden, like Western culture's other Edenic public space, the Athenian agora, turns out to be a minefield." After the snake lures them to eat what is forbidden, Adam and Eve survive divine malice. But they get "kicked out of Eden's phony open space." Now, the world is before them. Suddenly, they have to create a new world for themselves. They've become a "primal couple," Marshall said, "the world's first *refugees*." They've also enacted the world's first *solidarity*. "Expulsion, God's last gift, inspires them with the desire to create a garden of their own."

These were amongst the last words Marshall uttered. Lovely words. Timely words. His secular romantic vision, wrestling with the Bible, propels itself into our own times, perhaps coming closer to home than even Marshall himself imagined. In the Old Testament, "cities of refuge" were set aside as sanctuaries for people, spaces of asylum to protect the innocent (and sometimes the guilty): "These towns will be cities of refuge," the Book of Numbers said, "for the sons of Israel as well as for the stranger and the settler amongst you." The Hebraic tradition recognizes the right to an urban immunity and hospitality that goes beyond particularism, beyond a search for unique refuge: it's a divine hope for everyone, for a form of urban life and sovereignty where people can become wholly human.

Fast forward several thousand years. A number of American cities—Austin, Boston, Chicago, Los Angeles, New York, Oakland, Philadelphia, Providence, and San Francisco—all now pledge not to cooperate with their president's promise to deport millions of illegal immigrants. Across the US, "sanctuary cities" are gearing up to oppose the federal government and its immigration agents. Other liberal urban bastions reaffirm their intention to defy the national government. At the risk of losing millions of dollars in federal support, they've said—with varying degrees of firmness—their cities will act as bulwarks against mass deportation. These cities have no power to bestow "official" rights to people; but they have the power to resist, putting a new twist on struggles against federal government: this time it's liberal cities not conservative states who counter what they see as unjust national-level intervention. In response to a profound crisis of political legitimation, the specter of urban solidarity looms.

Maybe we can read Marshall's posthumous Biblical work as his own paean to the "city of refuge," his final dream-thought for a new status for the city, a new right *to* and *of* the city, a will to talk about the city, a will to live for the city. Can we ever reimagine the city giving us both spiritual rewards and political re-enfranchisement? Marshall hinted at an urban citizenship where people don't "let it be," where we refuse to be moved on—whether by beat cops on the street or ICE agents at the door. Marshall's endgame here can never be his final curtain call. He leaves us with a new beginning, a genesis. For his dying for the city can become *our* living for the city, our romance with the city, with public space, a yearning for a "place for us," somewhere that safeguards the downtrodden and disaffected and which offers asylum "for the stranger and settler amongst us." Now we all have someone and something to live up to, to follow: the Upper West Side's great bearded prophet who reimagined—as he said, as a conclusion to his life—"a renewed garden of Eden that will be open, and shared, and that will really be a public work."

There are days when I feel as if I've been kicked out of the Garden of Eden, kicked out of New York. I ate the forbidden fruit and paid the price. There are days when I think, *did I get forced out or force myself out?* Who knows, maybe Adam asked himself the same question. I've tried to create a new life beyond New York, after New York, tried to find my own place, with Corinna, as a couple, dealing with our paradise lost. Did our leaving help us enlarge ourselves? Was it like John Milton said, when he wound up his famous epic poem, *Paradise Lost*, from 1667, with these refrains: "To leave this Paradise, but shalt possess / A paradise within thee, happier far." "The world was all before them," Milton had said of Adam and Eve, "where to choose." "They hand in hand, with wandering steps and slow / Through Eden took their solitary way." The joy of being a human couple, Marshall had said, seeming to agree with Milton, is worth the loss of any Eden. To be together, in love, was to overcome, even to overcome the city, to reach out to your partner when everything else has been lost. To find your solitary way, together.

I know I should get over it, but there are days when my nostalgia for a paradise lost hurts. It gnaws away inside me, like a sickness, an aching sickness. This nostalgia seems to happen on gray days, on slow days, on lonely days, days when it rains, days when I feel depressed. At such moments, I wonder why I ever left New York, came back to a gloom of Britain that I had tried long ago to escape. And had succeeded! I'd made it out, fulfilled my ambition, got to New York. Though for some…some inexplicable reason...I left, quit it. There was an explicable reason, of course, but that was then. Now, the explanation has faded, failed me. I've forgotten why I left, why I did hate New York when now I miss it so terribly. It pains me to hear anybody talk about it, to see it on the TV, on film, on somebody's sweatshirt, anywhere.

At such moments, too, I hear my own Birdman voice inside my head, tormenting me as it had tormented Riggan Thomson, that Carver castoff: *"How did we end up here? This place is horrible. Smells like balls. We don't belong in this shit hole…"* No, I can't bear to see anybody else claim New York. That town is mine. New York is *my lost property*. I can never retrieve what's been lost and some days I feel the pain rile my whole body. In the mornings, as soon as I open my eyes, I can tell instantly whether today will be a New York lost property day, a day of yearning for lost time, knowing it's long gone, never to be reclaimed, that I decided to give it away, leave it behind. I can never bathe in the same waters twice. My New York lost property days are days of ruination, workless days. I can't write about anything other than New York. It haunts me when I am walking around, hearing Birdman voices. Only where I am, there are usually few people about, and nobody to wail to. I even try to keep this nostalgia, this aching, from Corinna. She doesn't understand why I still harbor it and nor do I.

On bad New York lost property days I like to re-watch *My Dinner With André*, at home, on DVD; no blockbuster movie house will ever stage this arthouse delight. The beginning and end of *My Dinner With André* incorporate my own found and lost New York, my own beginning and apparent end. At the film's start, remember Wally trudging through a rundown, graffiti-splattered Lower Manhattan, with litter everywhere. It's the early 1980s and he's looking dejected, in his trench-coat, crossing Canal Street, bemoaning the plight of his writer's life. When he was young, his inner voice-over says, he was an aristocrat, raised on the Upper East Side, surrounded by comfort. All he used to think about then was art and literature. Now, as middle-age looms, all he thinks about is *money*. This ideal of the struggling artist, working over his art while working over himself, out on a New York street, has had a powerful pull on me, really helping define my whole adult life. That was what I wanted to do, still want to do, and where

I wanted to do it. My problem was...is...I never think about money. I still only ever think about art and literature. Hence my nostalgia for Wally, for that beautiful opener to *My Dinner with André*, which bowls me over each time with passionate yearning, with passionate regret, reminding me what I used to yearn for. But watching it makes me feel better because I know this yearning can't stop.

In the film's finale, Wally treats himself to a cab—which is how me and Corinna remember it, too, *treating* ourselves to a cab sometimes, after a late night out. Wally stares out of the cab's window like a little boy. He is a little boy again, looks it, with that magical glint of wonderment in his eyes. As the city flashes by, so does his life. Erik Satie's "Gymnopédie No. 1" plays its sparse melancholic notes, under Wally's voice-over. Moments earlier, André had pondered on life's brevity, on its apparent meaningless, on the sudden rush of the cataract of time. "What does that mean? A wife. A husband. A son. A baby holds your hands, and then suddenly there's this huge man lifting you off the ground, and then he's gone. Where's that son? You know?" Then the city streets rush by Wally in the cab. "I rode home through the city streets," he says. "There wasn't a street—there wasn't a building—that wasn't connected to some memory in my mind. There, I was buying a suit with my father. There, I was having an ice cream soda after school…" What's lost, what's gone, memory in the mind. It was enough for me to bawl my eyes out.

Every time I return, go back to New York as a tourist, I'm always overwhelmed with sorrow and joy; the two emotions tug away inside me, interchange within me by the second. Being back on its streets again, experiencing a sensual familiarity of smells and sounds, of shafts of light, of fire trucks and police sirens, of phenomena beyond anything thought, anything cerebral, fills me with ecstatic joy; only an instant later I spoil it all by letting my head think, reminisce, wonder why did I leave, why did I go, why did I walk out on our relationship? This prevents me from being absolutely present, from being just there, with all the simple pleasures of everyday life, the gift that, gee, isn't this terrific, aren't you a lucky man to be here now, if only for a few days. Make the most of it. Enjoy it my friend!

I remember one time enjoying it, walking across Central Park, going via the reservoir as I used to, strolling counter to the flow of joggers. I ended up near the Guggenheim on the east side of the park. It was a wonderful crisp, chilly fall day, brilliant blue sky, everything quivered with autumnal color; even the light reflecting off the buildings on the West Side had a beautiful soft, golden hue. I felt as if I were floating above the ground. Near a Fifth Avenue exit in front of me was a standalone tree.

Its leaves were so red it looked like it was literally ablaze, on fire, glowing with embers. I stopped to look at this tree, watching its color radiate through me, thinking HOW WONDERFUL! That's all. HOW WONDERFUL! It was an unbelievable feeling, almost religious, a feeling of recognizing everything, of being connected to everything, like Whitman in "Song of Myself," being aware of the reality and the specialness of even the most mundane things. Its atoms are my atoms, what I am it is.

I've been back several times with my daughter and we've marveled together at New York's energy. She's old enough to feel it, and to enjoy it, not to be too intimidated by it. She tells me that, because she's studying drama at school, and loves it, she wants to be a famous actress. I tell her that maybe she should come and study in New York, and when she finds stardom she should get a place in the Beresford or somewhere like it, near the park, somewhere grand. She agrees. Then I say that maybe she should remember to keep a spare room there so that old papa can come stay sometime, and that we can walk in the park together. Maybe we can let maman come, too. And we can take strolls by that red tree in the fall and I can rediscover New York in old age, before I die, see it one last time for a while as an old person, see it as wondrously as I saw it as a young boy. It's a new wish image, maybe, to return as an old man, relive a few scenes of times gone by, but mainly to live out new ones, fresh times ahead, as I shuffle to Zabar's café or revisit some old I. B. Singer haunts, including his Broadway Mall pigeons, should there be any left. When Corinna and I had found each other, and went to see New York as a pretext for my seeing Marshall, we always spoke about growing old together in New York, walking hand in hand, with wandering steps, slowly making our solitary way, along the open road. We'd vowed it at our marriage. And who's to say that won't happen, that the road isn't still open for us? Perhaps I can dream of New York in old age, anticipate it again, like before, only different, because now, somehow, I've learned a lot about myself. Perhaps I can turn this aching nostalgia into a positive future longing, a longing for the good old days to come.

I've been going at it for a long while now. I'm wondering if it's about time I should wrap this thing up. I remember how Louis Malle and André Gregory wrapped up *Vanya on 42nd Street.* They'd started it as a New York performance, on 42nd Street, with a jazz soundtrack, and police sirens, and Uncle Vanya drinking from an I LOVE NEW YORK cup; they'd started out before we even knew they'd started out, with Dr. Astrov and Marina casually chatting, before we realize it's Chekhov they were casually chatting, a seamless beginning, from street to steppe. At the end, it's simply the end, they stop; the rural Russian estate becomes

New York again, with a group of New York actors. Around the table, they look at each other, become more self-conscious than they were when acting. They quietly draw their papers together, play themselves again. The jazz riff recommences, just as *Vanya on 42nd Street* had begun. "Great!" says director André, re-entering the scene, putting his arms around his actors, smiling. The camera continues to roll even as the curtain goes down, or would have gone down if there'd been a curtain. It was like André had said all along: "Vanya is like a rehearsal that gets deeper and deeper until you forget it's rehearsal." "What can we do, Uncle?" Sonya wondered at very end. "All we can do is live," she says, answering her own question. "We will live through a long row of days," she says. "And through endless evenings. And somehow we'll bear up."

What I've written here feels like a rehearsal for something. Perhaps for the book I've always wanted to write about the city and love, about what we talk about when we talk about cities and love. What do any of us know about love anyway, Carver's Mel had said. It seems he said that a long while ago. When it comes to love, Mel thought, we're all rank beginners. Remember that's what Carver originally called his story: *Beginners*. "We say we love each other," Mel said—or rather "Herb" said, because Carver calls Mel Herb in *Beginners*—"and we do, I don't doubt it. We love each other and we love hard, all of us. You know the kind of love I'm talking about is that attraction to the other person, the partner, the plain everyday kind of love, love of the other person's being, the loving to be with the other, the little things that make up everyday love, the day-to-day caring about the other."

The kind of love I'm talking about is the love Carver puts into the old couple almost killed in a head-on car crash with a drunk driver. It's fifty-fifty, their odds of living. But they pull through, draw upon tremendous reserves, on a sheer will to live, to be with each other again. Herb (Mel) is the surgeon who operates on them, and later looks over them, watches them recover. Both are rigged up in bed, elevated, bandaged, the whole works, from head to foot, with just little eye holes and places for a mouth and nose. The old man, Henry Gates, recovers faster than his wife, Anna. She's the worse off. He gets depressed for the longest while. Herb wonders why he's getting depressed; she's gonna live, he's gonna live. They're both gonna live. Henry says he's depressed because they can't physically be together; she's in a separate room. He can't be with her every day. Henry says they've been married a half-century and only been apart two nights. "Imagine that," Herb says to his gin-drinking friends. "But, Jesus, he was lonely for her. I'm telling you he *pined* for her. I never knew what that word meant before, *pined*, until I saw it happening to this man. He missed her something fierce."

The couple live in a remote place in Oregon. In winter, there's nothing to do and it's cold. The snow piles up in drifts. There's just the two of them and sometimes they can't go out. Their kids have moved away long ago. Month in, month out, all they have is each other. Henry tells Herb what they do, how they entertain themselves. "We go to the dances each night," he says. Herb is perplexed. What? Dances? We play an old record player every night, Henry explains. We listen to our old records and dance with each other in the living room, he says. Every night. Sometimes it'll be snowing outside and below zero. But inside they dance together, in each other's arms, in their stocking feet, in the living room. And then they go to bed and sleep under lots of quilts, warm and peaceful till morning.

It's a funny twist on Carver's other story, "Why Don't You Dance?" Perhaps, then, this is what we need to talk about when we talk about love. Love over the long haul. Love that transcends everything and everywhere. You can do it no matter what, no matter where, even in your own living room. So perhaps Marshall was right with his bright idea that you can even fall in love at Starbucks. It didn't matter where I ended up so long as *we* ended up somewhere, me and Corinna, us as a couple, stayed together, the two of us up against the madness of the world, hoping our daughter might fend off this madness, too, grow up to find love herself, somewhere, with someone. Meanwhile, we can dance together in our own living room, dance inside our own heads, together, somewhere, somehow. And maybe when we're old, we can find a way to shuffle down some crowded street like I wouldn't mind doing, hand in hand, me and Corinna. And that Milton was right, that to leave this paradise meant our paradise shall be within, and happier far.

It's not like we haven't had our ups and downs. We've had our tense moments and fraught situations, yelling and bawling at each other, me screaming most, whole periods when I've been depressed and treated Corinna shittily, taking out my own frustrations and anxieties on her, my nearest and dearest. It's maybe because she's been *nearest* that has made it easier for me to take it out on her, my dearest. We've never been as steady as Henry and Anna were, nor as self-contained, simply content in each other's company, with each other's company. We're both intense and emotional, reactive and expressively involved in our own creative output. That has often put a strain on things. There have been times when we thought we weren't going to make it through, that we were going to go our separate ways, split apart. Yet somehow we've stayed together. I've tried to support her in her career, she in my downward slide, in my anti-career. But with her my downward slide has become my saving grace. I've found what I've really wanted to do with my life and she's helped me do it, protected and financed me so that I could do it, taking a lot of flak en route. You might say I've found my calling, been able to express myself, to think, as Wally had, *only* about art and literature, and of course about Corinna and my daughter. Me and Corinna have been at two with the world for so long and that together, well, it makes four against the world and the odds of our pulling through are now about even. I haven't told her yet of my ambition to return to New York in old age, with her, should she be willing. I'll work on her for a while. I've got time, can write a few more books, funny little things that nobody's gonna read, let alone see, maybe like this thing. My daughter still has a few years left of school. Before then, I'm gonna stay put, try to write this down better. I'm not sure anything here makes any sense. I'm starting to sound like I'm rambling, rambling even more than I've been rambling throughout, drunk like Mel or something, or is that Herb, a few too many gins with Jane Jacobs. I mean, I don't have to be drunk to say what I think, do I? I mean, I'm just talking, right?

Andy Merrifield is the author of ten books, including works on urbanism and social theory such as *The New Urban Question and Magical Marxism*, biographies of Henri Lefebvre, Guy Debord, and John Berger, a popular travelogue, *The Wisdom of Donkeys*, and a manifesto for liberated living, *The Amateur*. His journalism has appeared in *The Nation*, *Harper's*, *Adbusters*, *New Left Review*, *Dissent*, the *Brooklyn Rail*, and *Radical Philosophy*.